LIFE OF PYTHON

George Perry

Little, Brown and Company
Boston   Toronto

LIBRARY OF CONGRESS CATALOG CARD NO. 83-82674

FIRST AMERICAN EDITION

MU

*Published simultaneously in Canada
by Little, Brown & Company (Canada) Limited*

PRINTED IN THE UNITED STATES OF AMERICA

CONTENTS

Introduction	page 6
Birth	9
Michael Palin	44
Terry Jones	58
Terry Gilliam	72
John Cleese	86
Graham Chapman	100
Eric Idle	112
Monty Python	124
Pythonography	185
Picture Credits	192

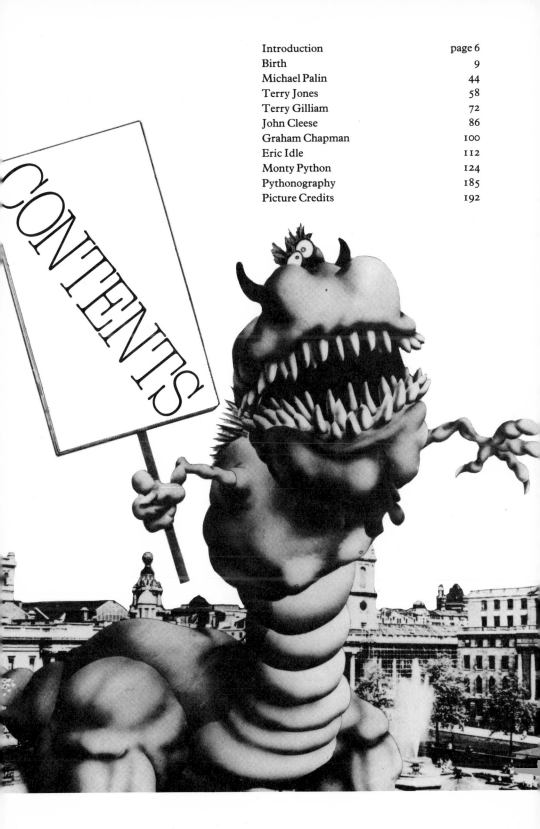

INTRODUCTION

THERE IS NO national monopoly on humour. Nevertheless, what one country finds funny can baffle another. Jokes translated from the Serbo-Croat rarely work in Wakefield or Waukegan. The British are as insular in humour as in most other things, and are not particularly adept at getting to grips with the things that make foreigners laugh. They pride themselves on their sense of humour and regard many other nations as deficient. Unquestionably, British comedy is unique. It is rich and diverse, and based on a robust tradition reaching back to the Middle Ages. Sadly, through the deficiencies of a century of bad teaching, schoolchildren often fail to appreciate just how hilarious is Chaucer. Shakespeare was as good at pithy one-liners as he was at refurbishing farcical plots lifted from the classics of his day. Dickens created an extraordinary gallery of great comic characters from Micawber to Fagin. English literature teems with comic writers of genius: Sterne, Congreve, Pope, Sheridan, Goldsmith, Thackeray, Austen, W.S. Gilbert, Lewis Carroll, Lear, Shaw, Wilde, Wodehouse, to name only a few, and if the Hibernian element seems unduly strong it serves to show that however divided politically, Ireland's legacy to Eng. Lit. is monumental.

Such a vigorous literary and theatrical heritage has enabled British humour to be more idiosyncratic than that of many other countries. American humour derives far more from the homogenising of a multiplicity of cultures under one flag; the coming together of British, Irish, French, German, Italian, Greek, Jewish, Hispanic, Negro, Eurasian, Chinese, Polynesian, Amerind and countless other cultures. It is hardly surprising that the Americans are the funniest people on this planet. That is, after the British.

It doesn't need an Aristotle to indicate that the number of basic jokes is finite, and that comedy is based on infinite variations on a handful of themes. Laughter is mankind's safety valve, the means by which hard times become endurable, arrogance is deflated, human weaknesses revealed. The great clowns can tell us much about the condition of man. They also give us a chance to enjoy ourselves. "Laughter is the great release," said musician George Harrison. He had in mind the team of comedians who emerged mostly from the ancient universities of Oxford and Cambridge in the 1960s and at the end of that decade banded together as Monty Python. They represent a high-water mark in the development of British humour, with a following around the world.

All are now in their forties and, as the grip of middle age tightens, they have had the compensation of fulfilling ambitions outside the group. As their most recent film, *Monty Python's The Meaning of Life*, demonstrates, the group has not mellowed; they are just as abrasive, irreverent, cynical and outrageous as they were in the days of their weekly television show, *Monty Python's Flying Circus*. What is remarkable about them as a team is that they are not natural show-business types. Former great comic groups – the Crazy Gang, the Marx Brothers etc. were vaudevillians, born in trunks, raised on the smell of greasepaint. But for various accidents the Pythons would have emerged from their universities to swell the ranks of doctors, lawyers, academics and admen. It has to be said that there are many people around who would rather it had been so, detesting the Python style of humour – its excesses, its bad taste, its refusal to follow conventional comic structures. The Pythons don't respect sensitivities, and delight in baiting self-appointed moralists. They have heard critics discuss their work in the same breath as Brueghel and Rabelais, Bosch and Grosz, Ruskin and the Brothers Grimm. They have entertained thousands at a time in such places as the Hollywood Bowl, where frenzied acclaim has greeted each favourite number as they reprise *Monty Python's Greatest Hits*.

Individually each is gifted and secure in his personal achievement. Together there is a synergism at work which produces a comic genius. A young writer in a dismissive review of *The Meaning of Life* in the *Monthly Film Bulletin* referred to them as "Grand Old Men". What is now coming to pass as time moves on is that they are becoming as cherished a British institution themselves as those that over the years they have tried so resolutely to deflate.

GEORGE PERRY
London, June 1983.

Acknowledgements

There are many people who have helped make this book, either by giving interviews, their time, advice or encouragement. Although it is by no means an official, authorised Python work, each member of the group went out of his way to be helpful, not only allowing generous interview time, but lending valuable and personal memorabilia which had not been published before. I am deeply grateful to Graham Chapman, John Cleese, Terry Gilliam, Eric Idle, Terry Jones and Michael Palin for making the task such a pleasant one. Among others interviewed I am grateful to Humphrey Barclay, George Harrison, Iain Johnstone, Charles Alverson, Barry Took, Peter Thompson, John Goldstone. Humphrey Barclay, John Tomiczek and Neil Innes were particularly helpful in supplying material at short notice. I am indebted to Anne James and the staff of the Monty Python office for their ready co-operation, and to Nancy Lewis in New York. The British Film Institute was, as ever, immensely helpful in providing background information and pictures. The Pythonography by Lucy Douch has been expanded from the BFI publication *Monty Python and the Theory of the Grotesque*. The professionalism of Vincent Page, who conducted the picture research, was unflagging. The staff of Pavilion Books, particularly Linda Martin, made the project possible, but the inspiration and enthusiastic encouragement of Colin Webb was the mainspring, and it is a fortunate author to have such a publisher. Lawrence Edwards designed the book with his characteristic flair. My agent, Pat White gave me constant support and counsel. My special gratitude is reserved for my wife, Frances, who worked arduously on the manuscript revision with me, and bore the project with patience and devotion, and to our six-year-old son Matthew, to whom Monty Python already means much.

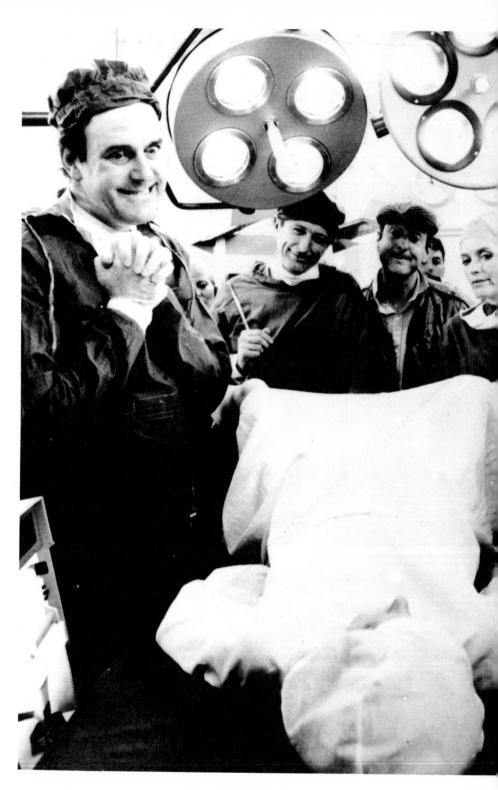

BIRTH

BRITISH HUMOUR BY AROUND 1950 was, to put it simply, dependent on three media – print, film and radio. The arrival of cheap printing in the nineteenth century had not only led to the wide dissemination of novels, newspapers, magazines and humorous periodicals such as *Punch* and its long-vanished imitators, but had enabled George Newnes to launch his halfpenny weekly *Comic Cuts*, ancestor of the *Dandy* and *Beano* and hundreds of other juvenile funny papers, many of which were still going decades later. Live entertainment then included another nineteenth-century innovation, the music hall or variety theatre, in which a succession of acts were performed in an unrelated sequence. Its traducer, the cinema, had purloined most of its great comedians from such a background, known as vaudeville in the United States, and some of the greatest, such as Charlie Chaplin, Stan Laurel and the less well-remembered Lupino Lane were British. To their names must be added those whose reputations were formed and flourished on their home turf, but who also came from the boards – Gracie Fields, George Formby, Will Hay. The third prong of popular humour, radio, was in 1950 still popularly known as the wireless. Broadcasting in Britain began in 1922, and for its first two decades was excessively dominated by the fiercely Calvinist figure of Lord Reith, the BBC's founding father and Director-General. Until the end of the thirties such humour that found its way into programme schedules tended to be whimsical, middle-class, genteel or lifted straight from the music hall, and indeed that was the title of the most listened-to Saturday-night show. Situation comedies and shows built around comic personalities, common enough in the United States, did not appear on the BBC until 1938 and *Band Waggon* with Arthur Askey and Richard Murdoch, and *It's That Man Again* with Tommy Handley in the following year, which also saw the start of the Second

World War and the transformation of British radio.

Wartime Britain was able to tune in to Jack Benny and Bob Hope, relayed by the BBC to amuse the troops, but listened to avidly by a civilian population unused to such formats. There were many home-grown counterparts, among them Handley's show, now known as *ITMA*; *Hi Gang!* with the transplanted Americans, Bebe Daniels, Ben Lyon and Vic Oliver; *Happidrome*; *Merrygoround* and many others. When the war ended there could be no going back, and new comedy shows emerged from the old. *Much-Binding-in-the-Marsh* with Kenneth Horne and Richard Murdoch for instance, was based on the Royal Air Force component of the tri-service *Merrygoround*. Tony Hancock first became a household name in *Educating Archie*, in which the leading character was a ventriloquist, (such was the power of radio on the imagination). Archie Andrews was the British equivalent of the biggest wooden radio star in the world, Charlie McCarthy, whose master was Edgar Bergen. But then, as early American listeners to Major Bowes would know, tap dancers, and even jugglers could be found places in schedules. Radio also developed the talents of a new breed of comedians, many of whom had become entertainers while serving in the armed forces. Peter Sellers, Frankie Howerd, Charlie Chester, Harry Secombe, Jon Pertwee, Michael Bentine, Spike Milligan, Jimmy Edwards, Arthur Haynes, Max Bygraves and many others became famous during this period.

Nowadays it is easy to forget the enormous influence radio comedy had in Britain. When Tommy Handley died suddenly in 1949, after ten seasons of *ITMA*, the sense of grief that prevailed was almost on the scale of that on the passing of King George VI three years later. Television, which the BBC had begun with the world's first regular high-definition service in 1936, remained off the air from 1939 until 1946. It had still not caught on as a popular medium, and would not do so until after the BBC monopoly was broken by the advent of Independent Television in 1955. Radio was still the predominant entertainment medium, and schoolchildren of the fifties, a group embracing all the Pythons, were avid listeners.

There are two BBC shows which made the most profound impression. The first was called *Take It From Here*, and much of its success stemmed from the fact that it was moved in to the programme slots previously filled by *ITMA* when that show came to a sudden end with the death of its star. Its stars were an Australian couple, the lugubrious Dick Bentley and the effervescent Joy Nichols, and Jimmy Edwards, a Cambridge Master of Arts and ex-RAF flier, winner of the DFC. At the university before his war service he had been a member of the famous Footlights Dramatic Club. The writers were another

Right, *Richard 'Stinker' Murdoch and 'Big-Hearted' Arthur Askey in the BBC's* Band Waggon, *1938. Below,* Tommy Handley flanked by Molly Weir, Lind Joyce and Diana Morrison who played his gorgon secretary, Miss Hotchkiss, *ITMA, 1946.*

Above, *Jimmy Edwards, Joy Nicholls and Dick Bentley in* Take It From Here, *1948.*

new team, Frank Muir and Denis Norden, who were particularly skilled at parodying movies and bringing topical events into their scripts.

The other radio programme which was to have a major effect on the course of British humour was *The Goon Show*, which began modestly in 1951 as *Crazy People*. It brought together Peter Sellers, who had made his name as an impressionist on the Ted Ray programme *Ray's a Laugh*, Harry Secombe, who had followed Max Bygraves and Tony Hancock in *Educating Archie*, and two other comedians who were getting their first big radio break, Spike Milligan and Michael Bentine. *The Goon Show* was anarchic, surrealist, manic, presenting a gallery of extraordinary characters – Eccles, Neddy

Left, Tony Hancock's radio break came with Educating Archie, *1951. Later, (right) Sidney James took over the role of tutor to Peter Brough's egregious doll, Archie Andrews. Above, Richard Murdoch and Kenneth Horne, stars of* Much Binding *with Dora Bryan, 1953.*

Seagoon, Moriarty, Bluebottle, Major Bloodnock, Henry and Minny in a succession of mind-addling plots week by week, each climbing new heights of the absurd. *The Goon Show* held its own in radio comedy all through the fifties, even as television was steadily encroaching, and ensnared the young in its web of lunacy, particularly at the universities, where it became a sacred cult, with even Prince Charles, heir to the throne, a novitiate.

In the fifties there still prevailed an attitude of deference to authority, respect for royalty, an unquestioned acceptance of the major institutions of Britain: the church, the law, Parliament, the public schools, the armed services, the ancient universities of Oxford and Cambridge. The British people meekly accepted the harshness of the years following the Second World War, and the limited aspirations that went with the ambitious creation of a welfare state, the nationalisation of key industries, stringent exchange con-

trols and the intrusion of bureaucracy in almost every corner of life. The postwar Labour government achieved a monumental social change in the face of appalling difficulties, but the electorate, having narrowly returned it in the 1950 election with a majority of only six, seized the opportunity in the following year to send back the Conservatives, led by Winston Churchill, who had promised a bonfire of controls and to "set the people free". It was the beginning of a new attitude, the ending of all the food rationing by 1954, the setting-up of commercial television in the following year, the start of an age of materialism, with the hard-pressed factories pouring out washing machines, refrigerators, TV sets, record players, cars, for a country that behaved as though it had only just discovered the existence of such things. The dementia that gripped certain groups of teenagers when an uninspired movie called *Rock Around the Clock* was released, causing them to denude the

Far Left, *The Goons – Spike Milligan, Peter Sellers and Harry Secombe – celebrate St David's Day.*
Left, *Goon fancier Prince Charles takes part in a Trinity College, Cambridge revue, 1969.*
Below, *Release of the movie,* Rock Around the Clock,

Bamber Gascoigne's Cambridge revue, Share My Lettuce, *transferred to the West End, 1957. Left to right: Philip Gilbert, Kenneth Williams and Barbara Evans.* Below, *Jonathan Miller, star of the Footlights 1954 revue* Out Of the Blue.

cinemas where it was shown of their seats, was attributed not as much to the hypnotic effect of rock 'n roll, but to the diminution of moral values that went with a new age of plenty.

In the autumn of that same year of 1956, however, there occurred the event which more than any other in the period since 1945 was the watershed – the moment when the edifice of the Establishment sustained permanent cracks. Suez was a great historic muddle, a debacle from which Britain emerged with little honour. The intervention of British troops at the instigation of Sir Anthony Eden's government drove rifts across political boundaries, even within the cabinet itself. As a Cambridge undergraduate at the time I remember vividly the protest marches, Tony Benn, then plain Anthony Wedgwood-Benn, shouting above the hubbub in a packed Union debating chamber, police separating pro- and antifactions with vigour during a demonstration on the large greensward, Parker's Piece.

It was not only the political life of Britain that came under scrutiny. In literature, America had its new generation of beatniks, Britain its "angry young men". It was an easy label attached by Fleet Street to any novelist, playwright or poet who adopted a knocking posture. Today, many of those who found themselves grouped in this category scarcely seem to be subversive critics. They included novelists John Braine, John Wain, Alan Sillitoe and even Kingsley Amis, critics Colin Wilson and Lindsay Anderson, late of the Oxford film magazine *Sequence*, and a number of playwrights led by John Osborne, whose now dated period piece *Look Back in Anger* had, after a spirited intervention by Kenneth Tynan, then drama critic of *The Observer*, turned Sloane Square into a rival of Shaftesbury Avenue. That autumn of 1956 the smell of grapeshot hung heavily in the air.

Cambridge saw at that time the emergence of a breed of undergraduates with new professional motivations, their sights firmly set on the media and the arts. The small, but excellent Amateur Dramatic Club Theatre in Park Street was the place in which Peter Hall and Trevor Nunn cut

their teeth. Bamber Gascoigne staged a revue with an odd title, *Share My Lettuce*, which transferred to the West End for a long run with a new cast that included Maggie Smith and Kenneth Williams, while its author still continued his studies at Magdalene. Michael Frayn in his first term won a large prize in an *Observer* copywriting contest, the first paid recognition of his comedic gifts. The 1954 Footlights Revue, *Out of the Blue*, had transferred to the Phoenix, and London had gone wild about a St John's medical student the twenty-year-old Jonathan Miller who attracted comparison with Danny Kaye, to the bafflement of his friends.

The Footlights are a Cambridge tradition without an Oxford equivalent. The club was founded a century ago, in 1883, and in its early years staged musical comedies of a localised kind. Less formal concerts would also be given, called "smokers", which took place usually within college walls and in front of all-male audiences. Soon after the First World War the annual show, staged for that glorious post-exam fortnight in Cambridge known as May Week although it takes place in June, followed the new revue format, some time after such entertainments had proved popular in the West End. Apart from what was regarded as a disastrous inclusion of women in the 1932 revue, the Footlights remained an all-male preserve until the 1960s. There was a perverse fascination in the sight of hairy-chested young men togging themselves up as flappers, with copious applications of rouge and mascara, and it became an essential part of the Footlights tradition. Jack Hulbert and his brother Claude appeared in Footlights' shows just before and after the First World War, as later did Richard Murdoch and Jimmy Edwards, but few people outside the University were aware of the club's existence.

Leslie Bricusse devised and produced *Out of the Blue* and among its writers was Frederic Raphael. Both of them were to pursue successful careers. The same team wrote *Lady at the Wheel*, a production for the Musical Comedy Club. Another star at the time was future Liberal MP John Pardoe, who wrote and performed in *The*

Girl Next Door and was in the 1955 Footlights show, Between the Lines, which also had a brief West End run. If Cambridge now seemed to have a direct line to Shaftesbury Avenue it also had its own Grub Street, in those days located in the narrow alleyway leading off King's Parade, called St Edward's Passage. There the offices of the weekly newspaper Varsity, a self-financing organ which flourished without any grants or subsidies, had its offices on the ground floor and dank basement of a shabby building backing on to the Arts Theatre. In such surroundings the careers of Nicholas Tomalin and Michael Winner, Gavin Lyall and Ron Hall were launched, and it became a rewarding enterprise to feed Fleet Street with Cambridge stories, the resulting revenue eking out the modest state student grant. Varsity, a lively tabloid, its style and appearance changing each term with the election of a new editor, was counterbalanced by the more upmarket glossy magazine Granta which had achieved national attention in 1953 when its then editor, Mark Boxer, was rusticated for blasphemy of all things, thus finding himself sharing a distinction with the poet Shelley who was sent down from Oxford for a similar offence in 1811.

The 1957 Footlights revue, called Zounds, which was directed by Graeme McDonald, now a senior figure at the BBC, broke new ground by having two women in the cast, which also included Joe Melia, Bob Wellings and Timothy Birdsall, a brilliant cartoonist as well as entertainer, and whose comic strips Rick Runcorn and Christopher Crumb enlivened the pages of Varsity. In the 1959 show, The Last Laugh directed by the brilliant John Bird, he appeared with Eleanor Bron, Bird agreeing with McDonald that the days of drag should be ended. Also in the cast was Peter Cook. The importance of the show was that instead of trotting out the customary sparkling musical numbers, polished revue sketches and blackouts, targeted at television performers and showbiz celebrities, it followed a polemical line, uncompromisingly going for a political attack. Sudden change always upsets the traditionalists, and they turned up to boo the opening night. Yet the show was the direct precursor of Beyond the Fringe, That Was the Week That Was and for that matter, Monty Python's Flying Circus, as we shall see. Willie Donaldson, who had become a vaguely entrepreneurial figure while he was still at Magdalene, having run a joint magazine called Gemini with Julian Mitchell at Oxford, staged a new version of The Last Laugh with a professional cast that included Sheila Hancock, Cleo Laine, Valentine Dyall and Lance Percival, and retitled it Here is the News. Unfortunately after a few weeks on tour it faded away, never making it to the West End. In the following year, Peter Cook, now in charge of the Footlights, returned to frivolity with Pop Goes Mrs Jessop.

Peter Cook, of Pembroke College, was one of the Oxbridge humorists most affected by The Goon Show and rapidly discerned depths of meaning within it that had escaped the BBC hierarchy. He perfected a deadpan technique and a monologue style which would lead to the creation of the curious rain-coated nutter known as E.L. Wisty. Such was the mesmeric intensity of this creation that for several terms after Cook's departure it was irritatingly faddish for undergraduates to adopt the Wisty voice. Cook could also construct apparently effortless parodies of Harold Pinter dialogue, with repeated phrases gradually tipping the sketch into total lunacy. Michael Codron, the young West End producer who had earlier brought Share My Lettuce to the West End invited Cook to write some items for a revue called Pieces of Eight, the principal author of which was in fact to be that same Harold Pinter. Cook, too, achieved the West End while still an undergraduate. He followed in 1961 with another Codron revue called One Over the Eight. But perhaps unwittingly Cook had already been partly responsible for killing off this particular kind of entertainment. The so-called intimate revue, once a mainstay of the West End, vanished during the sixties, and has never successfully been revived.

All male Cambridge Footlights c. 1890. Below, Cambridge Footlights 1964, by now the women are real.

The turning point was a show that was staged at Edinburgh during the run of the 1960 Festival. In addition to the main official attractions, a tradition had grown up for peripheral events to be staged that, although unconnected with the Festival programme, supplemented it and enabled small groups to appear before audiences and often indulge in experimentation. The universities were accustomed to sending not only their leading drama companies, but also tiny groups who would perform in the most unlikely venues. Such activity was known as the Fringe. In 1960 the Festival organisers themselves felt that they could stage an official revue as part of the main programme. The inspiration came from John Bassett, lately an undergraduate entrepreneur at Oxford, who had become the assistant to Robert Ponsonby, then the administrator of the Edinburgh Festival. At Oxford he had acted as agent and fixer for such events as Commem Balls, and one "client" was an organ scholar at Magdalen who not only could play good piano jazz, but had a quick line of repartee. Being of diminished height, he used that physical attribute to present an air of attractive cheek. He was Dudley Moore. Another performer on his books was Alan Bennett, of Exeter College, who had started writing funny sketches with Michael Frayn when they were doing their National Service and learning Russian together. Bennett, bespectacled and owl-like, offering an appearance of advanced middle age while still in his twenties, was a specialist at nonsense sermons and sustained speculative discourse. Bassett urged that he and Moore should form part of the Edinburgh revue, and in acknowledgement of the other university's known prowess, suggested teaming them with two Cambridge performers. The choice of Peter Cook was obvious enough, for he was the reigning star of the Footlights. Jonathan Miller, on the other hand, had gone down in 1956 and continued his medical training in

Alan Bennett, Dudley Moore, Peter Cook and Jonathan Miller, the Beyond the Fringe *team, Edinburgh 1960, with inset, Peter Cook as Harold Macmillan: 'A man can run a mile in four minutes.'*

London. By then he was a qualified doctor with no ambitions to pursue a theatrical career. The ambivalence of Dr Miller, poised between medicine and the arts, has continued from the day in 1960 when he was persuaded to become part of *Beyond the Fringe*.

The title, deliberately chosen to suggest that what was being done was not something of which the Fringe was capable, would in later years become as obscure as say, *The Clockwork Orange*, but would be taken for granted for its own sake. The show was presented with great simplicity, the emphasis being on the four performers rather than elaborate scenery and props. Their material consisted to some extent of old work that had gone well with university audiences, but it was beefed up with topical attacks on contemporary politics. Peter Cook impersonated Harold Macmillan lecturing the nation on its nuclear defence system and advising anyone foolish enough to consider the four-minute early warning inadequate that a man could run a mile in four minutes. The British war film was satirised as part of the process of demythologising the Establishment view of things. Cook as an RAF senior officer sends Miller to certain death telling him to raise the tone of the war with a futile gesture: "Get up in a crate, Perkins. Pop over to Bremen, take a shufti, don't come back. Goodbye Perkins." "Goodbye Sir – or is it – au revoir?" "No, Perkins." Other sketches attacked capital punishment, Beaverbrook-style journalism and Shakespearean production styles. Miller could unleash yards of bogus Bardic pentameters seemingly at will, delivered in a rhythm that accentuated its gibberishness:

"Get thee to Gloster, Essex. Do thee to Wessex, Exeter.
Fair Albany to Somerset must eke his route.
And Scroop, do you to Westmoreland, where shall bold York
Enrouted now for Lancaster, with forces of our Uncle Rutland,
Enjoin his standard with sweet Norfolk's host.
Fair Sussex, get thee to Warwicksbourne,

Beyond the Fringe *goes to Broadway, 1962.*

And there with frowning purpose, tell our plan
To Bedford's titled ear, that he shall press
With most insensate speed
And join his warlike effort to bold Dorset's side.
I most royally shall now to bed,
To sleep off all the nonsense I've just said."

Beyond the Fringe was a hit at Edinburgh and although he had not gone up to see it Willie Donaldson agreed to stage the show in London, in spite of having at the time severe cashflow problems following the failure of *Here is the News*. It opened at the Fortune Theatre for what was expected to be a modest run, but immediately received critical raves and it was regarded as the funniest production in most people's experience. Suddenly the word "satire" was the currency of the day. The Prime Minister, Harold Macmillan, even performed the masochistic exercise of going to see Peter Cook caricature him, and bravely bore it as befitted his carefully cultivated Supermac image, of which unflappability was the essence. Four relatively obscure young men basked in sudden and daunting fame. Far from being a short-lived phenomenon, the show was to go on running in London in one form or another until late in 1966. The original quartet stayed with it for the first year and then took it to Broadway, where it opened in October 1962, presented by Alexander H. Cohen. Many a British success has failed miserably on its Atlantic crossing, and some thought its chances slight since so much of it was local humour. How could Americans penetrate the various accents and class differences that permeated the show? As it happened, the show's Englishness, taken to a land where performers such as Mort Sahl, Mike Nichols and Elaine May, Bob Newhart and Shelley Berman had established a brand of pithy, crackling comedy, usually performed in late evening settings, proved to be an asset. In every season in New York there is a show that draws fashionable attention. In the fall of '62 that show was *Beyond the Fringe*.

Its success in Britain and America was a crucial factor in plotting the course of British comedy from that time onwards. More than two decades later the quartet

Peter Cook and Dudley Moore teamed up on television in Not Only . . . But Also, *1966.*

have gone their own ways to various other successes – Alan Bennett to becoming a sensitive, funny playwright of distinction, Peter Cook to a varied career as writer, actor and entertainer whose collaboration for some years with Dudley Moore included some notable television series such as *Not Only, But Also* and *Pete and Dud*. Dudley Moore subsequently migrated to California where he is now a Hollywood superstar on the strength of his film *Arthur*, but in danger of doing too many less successful follow-ups. Jonathan Miller, mercurial, brilliant, multi-talented, has conducted several careers as a television pundit, documentarist, TV, theatre and opera director, and now yet again has abandoned it all for medicine.

The effects of *Beyond the Fringe* went far. Just as "angry young men" had made the headlines five years earlier, Fleet Street now latched on to "the satirists". A new generation of young men, mostly from the two leading universities, spread their net. An Oxonian, Richard Ingrams (having worked with a cartoonist called William Rushton on the Shrewsbury school magazine, *The Salopian*, and hav-

ing taken over *Parson's Pleasure*, an Oxford humour magazine, with another Salopian, Paul Foot) contributed to *Mesopotamia*, along with Andrew Osmond, John Wells and Rushton, who had not gone to the university. Its business spark was provided by Peter Usborne. In the summer of 1961, during the West End honeymoon of *Beyond the Fringe*, Usborne decided to attempt a satirical magazine for general circulation. Another old Salopian, Christopher Booker (who had been at Cambridge) was pulled in and he, Ingrams and Rushton brought out the first pilot edition of *Private Eye* in October. Usborne and Osmond were responsible for the business side, but the initial stages were shaky. Osmond departed for a Foreign Office career, leaving the problem of a backer for the regular publication of the paper. Peter Cook, known to have ambitions to produce his own humorous journal, was approached, and agreed to become the majority shareholder. *Private Eye* has combined malicious and frequently inadequate gossip, justifiable sneers at pretentious journalists (always "hacks" in Eye terminology) and puffed-up mediapersons, with a handful of triumphant exposés. There have been times when its angry targets have lined up at the Law Courts to sue for libel, and its long list of litigants includes Randolph

Above, *Peter Cook outside what was to become the Soho smart meeting place, The Establishment.* Right, *Persecuted American comedian, Lenny Bruce, arrives at Heathrow to appear at The Establishment.* Far right, *The first pilot issue of the satirical fortnightly,* Private Eye, *appeared in October 1961.*

Churchill, Sir James Goldsmith, Robert Maxwell, Desmond Wilcox and Harold Evans.

It would seem that *Private Eye*, certain individuals excepted, is the only enduring survivor of the 1961–2 so-called "satire boom". The Establishment nightclub, another of its manifestations, was a pet notion of Peter Cook, who had got the idea from political nightclubs he had seen in Europe, where he had spent a year prior to going to Cambridge. In partnership with Nicholas Luard who had been treasurer of the Footlights at Cambridge, he took a lease on a Soho strip club and engaged the services of the then most spectacular theatre designer, Sean Kenny, to create a suitable internal decor. Long before it opened for business The Establishment was a success, and charter memberships brought in sufficient revenue to carry out the Kenny designs. The intention was not only to present evening cabaret with a sharper bite than elsewhere in the West End, but to keep the place alive during the day with films, snacks, light lunches, and as a meeting place. John Bird directed the first show and several others, and the performers included many who had graduated from Cambridge and the Footlights, such as Eleanor Bron and John Fortune. Dudley Moore was accustomed to going along with Cook from the

performance of *Beyond the Fringe* and playing piano with his trio in the basement.

The Establishment's targets were not just the real Establishment, the names coined in the fifties to denote the pillars of British life such as Parliament, the law, the church, the armed forces and of course, Whitehall. Such objects of attack were often too easy to pick off. John Bird made a speciality of black African politicians, and Fortune and Bron became the British equivalent of Nichols and May, brilliantly lampooning middle-class woolly liberals. Cook's most notorious coup was to get the great, persecuted American comedian Lenny Bruce to appear, an engagement which roused the *Daily Express* to rage and the Home Office to action. The presence of large numbers of visitors from Scotland Yard observing the proceedings assisted the image of The Establishment as a forum of political criticism, and the appearances of Lenny Bruce proved to be immensely valuable in revealing the dark side of Presidents Kennedy and Johnson.

But its heyday was brief. After two years, financial control passed into other hands following a series of managerial disasters, and the tone of the place changed to that of one of Soho's tackier drinking spots.

To the amazement of many traditionalists, the British Broadcasting Corporation, for so long regarded as a stuffy bastion of the real Establishment, threw off its "Aunty" image, and leapt wholeheartedly on the back of the new trendiness. One man was responsible. In 1960 the Corporation had acquired a new Director-General, Hugh Carleton Greene, a large man in every sense. (His towering height equalled that of the afore-mentioned Reith, in whose image the BBC still made some obeisance.) His tenure coincided with an adventurous time for British television, a loosening-up of attitudes, particularly in the area of current affairs and drama. The days of the deferential political interview in which the questions were carefully prepared in advance, submitted with respectful genuflections by the asker, who would then not react to the inevitable platitudes but pass

onto the next question on the clipboard, were already ended in the mid-fifties. The change was due to the advent of Independent Television News with its more aggressive approach and interviewers such as Robin Day and Christopher Chataway (both of whom were recent graduates form Oxford). The BBC under Hugh Greene became more assertive and confident of its position, accepting the fact that while politicians may not like it, that there was a public duty to question and to criticise while remaining within the framework of balance demanded by the BBC Charter. Grace Wyndham Goldie, as formidable a figure as ever walked the corridors of the Corporation, gathered up her so-called young men, who breathed a new life into the face of television.

Peter Cook and John Bird had suggested that the BBC try a satire show, based on what was going on at The Establishment, but discussions proved abortive. Then the Current Affairs department, which since 1957 had run a nightly early evening magazine called *Tonight*, combining studio interviews with filmed reports and occasional sketches and musical numbers, was called upon by Greene to devise a late-night satire show. The Light Entertainment department was passed over, much to their disgust, but had, in any case, been unable to offer a satisfactory format. A *Tonight* producer, Ned Sherrin, was assigned the task of getting the new programme on the air. It is a matter of historic fact that the job of compering it was first offered to John Bird, who preferred to turn it down, although he was quite willing to perform in the cast. So Sherrin looked round at other graduates who were trying to make their way in show-business. One of them was David Frost, another ex-star of the Footlights, who had been working with the weekday London ITV contractor, Associated-Rediffusion, on their current affairs programme *This Week*. He had been given a chance to present a short series based on the prevailing dance craze, the Twist, but he would be the first to admit that his onscreen debut was unremarkable. He was, however, augmenting his meagre salary by appearing occasion-

ally at The Establishment, and then at a club called The Blue Angel, where Sherrin saw him in action doing yet another impersonation of Harold Macmillan.

After a couple of pilots, solely for the purpose of determining the format, which were not transmitted, *That Was the Week That Was* went on the air on Saturday, 24 November, 1962, and thereafter became a fixture for the next six months. It was unlike any show that had been seen on TV before – a mixture of commentary, sketches, songs, blackouts, film, debate, and a glimpse of the Sunday papers. Today, it sounds scarcely different from breakfast television, but then it was amazingly fresh. Frost fronted the show from behind a desk and addressed the audience directly. Flanking him were the other regular performers, including William Rushton, Lance Percival, Roy Kinnear and redheaded singer Millicent Martin, whose nasal intonation of the title song, its lyric adjusted weekly to accommodate events, shot her to stardom. It was a live show and worked to a tight deadline so that sometimes it looked as though it was shaping before the cameras. Sherrin made no bones about hiding the mechanics of it. Cameras wheeled in and out of shot and the atmosphere of the studio with its many normally unseen technicians were as familiar to viewers as they were to the audience on the spot, who had been warmed up beforehand by BBC mulled wine.

For the first time that anyone could ever remember BBC airtime was used for attacking living people, sometimes those in authority. An early object of *TW TW TW*'s was the Home Secretary of the day, Henry Brooke, whose performance had been both undistinguished and inept. The techniques used were acceptable in Fleet Street but unprecedented on television. Facts would be assembled and presented straightforwardly, but by juxtaposition and commentary a powerful editorial position would be adopted. Bernard Levin, an articulate graduate of the London School of Economics, former lobby correspondent and drama critic, was given his own spot to sound off about any of his pet hobby-horses. On one occasion he was assaulted before the cameras by the disgruntled husband of a woman

The cast of That Was The Week That Was, *BBC Television's Saturday night satire show, 1962.*

singer it was felt he had unfairly maligned. Levin was built up as a man of trenchant and abrasive opinions, uncaring of popularity, who voiced unpleasant truths. *TWTWTW* also developed the talents of ex-Footlight Timothy Birdsall who could not only improvise brilliantly absurdist monologues, but illustrate them as he went along with butcher paper and a Magic Marker. Tim Birdsall was already established as a cartoonist on *The Sunday Times*, and his death from leukaemia in 1963 at the age of twenty-six was a tragic loss to graphics and to television.

The life of *TWTWTW* was short. Its first season lasted for twenty-three weeks, its second a mere fourteen. It became compulsive viewing for large numbers of people and even Saturday night social gatherings would come to a standstill so that it could be watched. It had the effect of rousing large sections to fury, and politicians particularly squirmed while it was on the air. Hugh Greene, aware that 1964 was to be the year for a general election decided that the show on 28 December,

1963 would be the last. At the time the axing of *TWTWTW* was seen as an instance of typical BBC pusillanimity; in retrospect it was clearly better for it to have ended while the team was still ahead. The American version of the show, again presented by David Frost, was less fortunate, and after early success it wilted. The resignation of Harold Macmillan as Prime Minister and leader of the Conservative party and his replacement by Sir Alec Douglas-Home had led to a memorable attack in October which had concluded with Frost saying: "And so, there is the choice for the electorate. On the one hand, Lord Home – on the other hand, Mr Harold Wilson. Dull Alec versus smart-alec." While the impartiality could be admired, such stuff would get increasingly dangerous as the election drew near, and the BBC, while traditionally independent from the government of the day, unlike national broadcasting authorities in most other countries, is nevertheless reliant on the largesse from the licence fee, the scale of which is determined by Parliament.

TWTWTW, for all the brilliant use it made of its performers, establishing most of them as personalities so closely associated with it that to this day it is the programme most associated with certain of them, was very much a writers' show, and as the end titles rolled, the list of contributors sometimes seemed endless. People from *Private Eye*, especially Christopher Booker who was about to be ousted from there in any case, were among them, as were playwrights such as Keith Waterhouse and Willis Hall, and older humorists such as Caryl Brahms, whom Sherrin commissioned to write the weekly update for the opening song. Her instant lyrics for the song Millicent Martin sang on the specially-arranged show that was assembled within twenty-four hours of the assassination of John F. Kennedy, were particularly admired. A name occasionally cropping up in the writers' credits was that of John Cleese, whose first manifestation outside Cambridge had been as

Left, *Programme of Humphrey Barclay's 1963 Footlights revue.* Right, *Jo Kendall and John Cleese in the 'Private Lives' spoof from the show.*

the pillar (in every sense in view of his 6' 5" height) of the 1963 Footlights revue, *A Clump of Plinths.* The show had been brought to the West End by a very youthful producer, Michael White, under the more manageable, and as it turned out, highly significant title, *Cambridge Circus*.

It ran at the Lyric in Shaftesbury Avenue after five weeks at the New Arts, opening on 16 August. Its director was Humphrey Barclay, newly graduated from Trinity, who was to go on to become a major force in television comedy.

"*Cambridge Circus* was only the second show Michael White put on," said Barclay. "We were all totally unshowbizzy then. Especially John. There was a bizarre logic about his humour – a strong element of fierce nonsense running through it. I was aware of it the first time I ever saw him at a smoker in the old Footlight premises off Lion Yard, alas no more, buried under the Petty Cury shopping precinct. John was so tall his head almost disappeared behind the proscenium arch – it was a very tiny stage – but he was amazing, he had this wonderful capacity for logical lunacy."

Among other performers in *Cambridge*

YORK FESTIVAL 1963

THE 1963 FOOTLIGHTS REVUE

'A Clump of Plinths'

A Clump of Plinths *transferred to the West End as* Cambridge Circus. Above, *David Hatch, Jo Kendall, John Cleese, Graham Chapman, Tim Brooke-Taylor, Bill Oddie and Chris Stuart-Clarke are moved on by a real constable from Cambridge Circus, 1963.* Below, *The long-running custard-pie demonstration gets an early airing in* Cambridge Circus.

Circus were Bill Oddie, Tim Brooke-Taylor, Jo Kendall, David Hatch, and Graham Chapman, who had graduated from Emmanuel in the preceding year and was now at St Bartholomew's Hospital furthering his medical studies. He had been called in by Barclay to replace Tony Buffery, a cast member who had given up the stage to pursue another career. When the run at the Lyric ended in November it looked as though each of them would go separate ways. But Barclay had by now landed his job at the BBC: "I failed to get a general traineeship. But there was a man called Peter Titheradge, who had been charged with the task of recruiting university talent. You see, with the success of *Beyond the Fringe* and *That Was the Week* Oxbridge humour was very much in vogue. We loathed this 'satire' tag, we

Tim Brooke-Taylor and John Cleese in I'm Sorry I'll Read That Again, *observed by Graham Chapman.*

were really into silliness. A very strong silly school had grown up and it was interesting to watch it develop – started I think by Peter Cook. The other powerful element was nostalgia for the music hall – that was the influence of Robert Atkins, who had been the Footlights president the year before Tim Brooke-Taylor. I was enormously influenced by him, and by Trevor Nunn. Anyway, Titheradge got me into the BBC – I was tremendously lucky, being around at exactly the right moment, and I became assistant radio producer."

He assembled some of the Cambridge Circus cast – Brooke-Taylor, Oddie, Hatch, Kendall and Cleese and recorded three shows under the heading *I'm Sorry, I'll Read That Again*, a sentence normally uttered by a newscaster who has muffed his lines. The material was drawn from a mixture of old and new, and the format was themeless, permitting a broad latitude of attack. In 1964 Michael White brought the *Cambridge Circus* team together again for a tour of New Zealand. The opportunity was such an unlikely one and the distance so great that most of them were sufficiently intrigued to agree to go.

Humphrey Barclay was given leave from the BBC and Graham Chapman dropped out from Bart's, delaying his qualifications as a doctor for a year. He was still unresolved as to whether he should pursue medicine or show-business as a final career, but had decided that he ought at least become a doctor before making the decision. During the *Cambridge Circus* West End run he had to be ready for the ward rounds at 8.30 am, but before that he had appeared in cabaret at The Blue Angel with David Frost, and had been unable to reach his bed until 3.30 am. He alleges that it was the Queen Mother who gave her blessing to his New Zealand trip. As secretary of the students' union he had been one of the privileged few to take tea with her during an official visit to the hospital. He had mentioned to her over a cucumber sandwich that he had been offered the New Zealand tour but that it would mean a few months off from his studies. The Queen Mother said "It's a beautiful place – you must go" and he interpreted this as a royal command.

It turned out to be a journey of some rigour – it was winter in the Antipodes, and New Zealand still preserves attitudes towards central heating that were commonplace in Britain in 1947 or so. The tour lasted six weeks and encompassed the major cities and the occasional small town. Much of it was uphill work, as the natives who turned up for the matinees were totally untuned to their style of humour. The hotels in which they stayed had their moments. John Cleese remembers with particular horror the occasion when Graham Chapman demanded a three-egg omelette for breakfast, and after several expressions of incredulity from the serving staff was brought an omelette with three fried eggs sitting on top of it.

During the tour an offer came through from New York to put *Cambridge Circus* on Broadway, under the patronage of the veteran producer Sol Hurok. *Beyond the Fringe* had blazed the trail for British university wits two years earlier, and there was a fashionable demand for such entertainment. They opened the show at the

Top left, The Cambridge Circus *company arrives in Dunedin, New Zealand. Top right, 'Judge Not', a famous sketch from* Cambridge Circus. *Centre,* Cambridge Circus *reaches Broadway, 1964. Bottom left, David Hatch and Graham Chapman in the New York production. Bottom right, Humphrey Barclay's cartoon of the* Circus *cast for* Varsity, *the Cambridge undergraduate weekly newspaper.*

WARM WELCOME TO OTAGO

LEFT TO RIGHT: Bill Oddie, John Cleese, David Hatch, Jo Kendall, Graham Chapman, Jonathan Lynn, Tim Brooke-Taylor.

This is a drawing (made especially for this celebration edition of Varsity) of the London-New York cast of "Cambridge Circus" by their director Humphrey Barclay. This was the record-breaking Footlights Revue of 1963, which spawned a group of comedians who have made an enormous mark on the entertainment scene since then. Between them they have created BBC Radio's "I'm Sorry, I'll Read That Again", BBC TV's "Twice A Fortnight", and Rediffusion's "At Last The 1948 Show" and "Do Not Adjust Your Set", four comedy shows which have broken completely new ground. Humphrey Barclay used to draw for Varsity and is now a TV producer (with Rediffusion).

Barclay

Plymouth Theatre on 6 October, 1964. A lukewarm review by a stand-in critic in *The New York Times* which was less generous than those in other newspapers was sufficient to limit the run to a mere three weeks. However, a niche was found off-Broadway, at the Square East in Greenwich Village where the atmosphere was more that of a cabaret, with the audience able to dine and drink while they watched the show. At the end of the year the Britons all left, and an American cast took over – something of an artistic mistake in view of the gulf between styles of humour in the two countries. While Graham Chapman returned to London to continue his medical studies, along with Humphrey Barclay and David Hatch to the BBC, Cleese stayed on in New York and briefly appeared in the show *Half a Sixpence*. Already a memorable meeting had occurred between John Cleese and Terry Gilliam, then working for little pay on an under-financed humour magazine called *Help!* which was published by Harvey Kurtzman. It ran photographed comic strips in the style of the Italian *fumetti* and Terry Gilliam, a cartoonist migrant from the West Coast, was charged with the job of finding interesting, but poor, actors who would pose for them. Cleese, as we shall see, was approached and duly appeared as a man in love with a Barbie doll, and received some $15 for his labours.

Tiring of *Half a Sixpence*, Cleese then spent five weeks working for *Newsweek* as a journalist, but found the experience less than satisfactory. He left and joined the touring company from The Establishment which was still going round the United States. John Cleese's restlessness is fundamental to his character, "Every day it seemed he had taken up something new," said Humphrey Barclay. "Always with tremendous enthusiasm. We laughed when one day he produced this American blonde and we said 'Today it's women'. Except, of course, it was Connie and he married her."

I'm Sorry, I'll Read That Again, having had three programmes broadcast in 1964, became a regular feature on BBC radio from October 1965. In fact, it was to stay on the air for some eight series which took it up to the winter of 1974, and thus became one of the BBC's most successful comedy shows, achieving a timespan as great as that of ITMA in the forties. The regular team was Tim Brooke-Taylor, Graeme Garden (who had replaced Graham Chapman), Bill Oddie, David Hatch, Jo Kendall and John Cleese, who returned from the United States in time for the second series in 1966. The first four series were produced by Humphrey Barclay but he then left to join the ITV programme company, Rediffusion. The show was immensely influential in that it developed the comic gifts of John Cleese, whose impressive personality dominated it, and was used as part of its appeal. Many of the jokes were of the slightly surreal Cleesian "ferret-up-the-nose" Footlights school of writing, but John also proved brilliant at creating bizarre Cowardesque sketches he would play with Jo Kendall, in the strangulated tones of a thirties posh accent. Bill Oddie was also a major asset, his musical invention and prolific output producing more than a hundred joke songs, which he performed often playing several instruments at once as well as singing. The audience subscribed to the cult of *I'm Sorry*, but each week the fans would gather in the Paris Cinema, BBC comedy's sub-basement studio two blocks south of Piccadilly Circus, to hiss, boo, applaud, shout and cheer, sometimes to the frustration of the performers until they learned how to use it to their advantage.

There was a gap between the seventh and eighth series of three years, and it was during the break that *Monty Python's Flying Circus* made its mark. Tim Brooke-Taylor, Bill Oddie and Graeme Garden also made an impact on television as *The Goodies,* and the others also established important careers – Hatch as head of BBC radio comedy, Barclay as Head of Comedy at London Weekend Television, Kendall (who had also been at Cambridge) as a top radio comedy actress.

Although Oxford has no equivalent of the Footlights, the theatrical strengths are

Michael Palin and Robert Hewison in Keep This To Yourself, *Oxford 1964. The girl in the niche is yachtswoman Clare Francis.*

as evident there as in the Fenland rival, and the long-lived Oxford University Dramatic Society (or OUDS) has nurtured many prominent careers. The Experimental Theatre Club has a tradition of staging revues, and both groups make a practice of sending productions to the Edinburgh Festival. As at Cambridge, smaller college clubs also provide opportunities for performing. In such an atmosphere a number of talents were sharpened in the early sixties, including those of Michael York, Clare Francis the round-the-world yachtswoman (who was then showing thespian skills) Miles Kington, Robert Hewison, Braham Murray, Paul McDowell who made a hit from the antique song *You're Driving Me Crazy* with a band called the Temperance Seven, and the two most outstanding humorists at the university, Terry Jones who was at St Edmund Hall, and Michael Palin at Brasenose.

The famous custard pie sketch in which a lecturer describes the essentials of humour while a trio of solemn demonstrators

Michael Palin (second right) and Michael York (far right) in an Oxford ETC drama production, 1962.

in overalls thrust carefully timed pastries into each other's faces, surfaced here, and was taken up by *Cambridge Circus* for their New Zealand tour, subsequently becoming a standard item in the Python stage repertoire. Terry Jones says that the original idea came from Bernard Braden, but it was he and Michael Palin who worked it out, and from that beginning formed a writing team of major importance.

In 1963 Terry Jones appeared in an Oxford Theatre Group revue which went to the Edinburgh Festival, and then had a short London run, initially of ten days at the LAMDA theatre, and then at the Phoenix, where it was played in front of drapes. Produced by Ian Davidson, it had the somewhat obscure title of ****, inspired no doubt by the celebrated Lady Chatterley trial a couple of years earlier. The cast consisted of Jones, Davidson, Doug Fisher, Robin Grove-White and Jane Brayshaw.

In the following year the ETC set itself

the difficult task of mounting a revue which took capital punishment as its theme. The approach was sub-Brechtian, raiding a number of published texts and dramatising them, and also using the voices of people tape-recorded in pubs, railway stations and streets, airing their views on an emotive subject. Old songbooks were culled for traditional material, and interpolations included *The Ballad of Timothy Evans* by Ewan McColl and *Strange Fruit*, a song immortalised by Billie Holiday. The tone of the piece was savage, ironic and polemical, and the cast, under Braham Murray's direction, proved equally as capable of ensemble performance as acting individually. Both Terry Jones and Michael Palin were in it, as was Palin's college mate, Robert Hewison. A bevy of Oxford beauties from the women's colleges were also featured. The prize was a West End run at the Comedy Theatre, presented by Michael Codron, who a few years earlier had staged Bamber Gascoigne's Cambridge revue *Share My Lettuce* at the same theatre. Gascoigne was now the drama critic of the *Sunday Telegraph*, and in his review he likened Terry Jones's white-faced mime with the artistry of Marcel Marceau. "Unfortunately," said Jones, "he mixed my name up with someone else in the cast, and attributed it to him!"

The collaboration of Palin and Jones continued through 1964, and they appeared in *The Oxford Revue* at Edinburgh (there seemed to be an Oxonian reluctance to follow the Cambridge pattern of giving their shows fanciful, obscure and irrelevant titles) with Doug Fisher, Nigel Pegram and Annabel Leventon. Jones went down from Oxford that year, Palin in 1965, after directing and appearing in *The Oxford Line*. Then he, too, was at loose in the world. They had mistakenly accepted an engagement at The Establishment, unaware that it was no longer the centre of the universe, and that after Peter Cook's long absence in America it had become one of Soho's tackier nightspots, with the audiences it deserved. Jones was commissioned by Willie Donaldson to write a musical about love, and on a modest retainer occupied a bedsit in Earls Court working out with Palin a

show based on the sexual revolution, which never reached the stage. He then found a pleasant job in the BBC as an assistant to Frank Muir, and from there he went to *Late Night Line-Up*, a nightly magazine show on BBC2. He was soon contributing sketches with Palin and Hewison for the Friday night edition, which was intended to be less serious than those earlier in the week, but friction occurred within the established hierarchy and they were axed.

"I realised that something was up when they no longer laughed in the control room," said Jones. "And then one day, Dennis Potter, the acerbic playwright, was being interviewed, and he said 'I didn't come all the way from Gloucestershire to appear alongside this tripe!'"

Once more David Frost hoved on to the scene. Terry Jones remembers during his brief time in the Light Entertainment department at the BBC watching the discussions that eventually resulted in a programme called *The Frost Report*. Frost

Mick Sadler and Michael Palin in Edinburgh for The Oxford Line, *1965. The lady in the casement is Diana Quick.*

had become an international star of some magnitude following the American version of *That Was The Week That Was* and its stage tour. After the 1964 General Election which had returned the first Labour Government for thirteen years (under the leadership of Harold Wilson) the BBC came up with a show appearing on Fridays, Saturdays and Sundays in a late-evening slot. It was called *Not So Much a Programme, More a Way of Life*, a Ned Sherrin title that sounded more like a song lyric. David Frost presided. The formula consisted of discussion between a number of people such as Bernard Levin, Labour MP Gerald Kaufman, philosopher's wife Dee Wells, an American agent called Harvey Orkin, and the brilliant stuttering humorist, Patrick Campbell, interspersed with sketches performed by John Bird, Eleanor Bron, John Fortune, P.J. Kavanagh and others. The balance, however, was tipped in favour of talk. The triple-night formula set up some

David Frost with the Frost Over England *cast: Julie Felix, Sheila Steafel, Ronnie Barker, John Cleese and Ronnie Corbett.*

strain (British TV has never been able to encompass successfully a nightly chat show on the lines of *Tonight* with Johnny Carson). *NSMAP, MAWOL* only lasted one season, and was regarded as a damp squib after the much-lamented *TWTWTW*. It did, however, prove a stepping stone for Frost, enabling him to become a talkshow host on American TV, and he duly took his place alongside Carson, Cavett, Griffin and the rest, establishing an unbeatable record in transatlantic commuting.

The Frost Report was a weekly series, with each programme dedicated to a humorous examination of a major topic. Those dealt with in the first series were authority, holidays, sin, elections, class, news, education and love, and in the second series, money, women, the forces, parliament, countryside and industry.

There was also a later special on Christmas at the appropriate time of the year. The main stars of the shows were Ronnie Barker and Ronnie Corbett, with Sheila Steafel, John Cleese and others abetting. A great many writers were needed, and Frost assembled them from all the principal sources. Anthony Jay welded the work into shape and provided the basic format. Contributors included Frank Muir and Denis Norden, co-writers of the old radio show *Take It From Here*, Dick Vosburgh, Barry Cryer, Keith Waterhouse and Willis Hall, David Nobbs, Barry Took and Marty Feldman. To this illustrious assembly of writers were added the names of John Cleese and Graham Chapman, and Terry Jones and Michael Palin. Also joining the team was Eric Idle, who was still at Cambridge after Cleese, Tim Brooke-Taylor, Bill Oddie and Graeme Garden had all gone down. With Idle an extraordinary era of the Footlights, which had begun eleven years earlier with *Out of the Blue* and Jonathan Miller (a star who was never a member), came to an end. Although later performers such as Clive James, Germaine Greer, Griff Rhys Jones and Douglas Adams became celebrated, the Cambridge link was less obvious.

Five of the six members of the future Monty Python team were thus brought together to work on *The Frost Report*, albeit as participators in a much larger group enterprise. Frost fronted the show with what became known in the jargon as the "Continuous Developing Monologue" or "CDM", to which Eric Idle and the others were required to contribute. Terry Jones recalls that they were paid a mere £7 per minute, and were lucky, given the input into the show, to average more than a couple of minutes in each one, which provided them with scarcely enough to live on. "After a while we were allowed by Jimmy Gilbert, who was the producer, to appear in some of our sketches," said Jones, "and that made all the difference because we could then get acting fees." They developed their talent for visual humour and learned how to set up jokes with economy in both a verbal and a logistical sense, a facility that was to prove immensely useful for the future.

Cleese and Chapman, the Cambridge team of writer-performers on *The Frost Report*, had been asked by Frost to collaborate on the screenplay of a film he was producing, *The Rise and Rise of Michael Rimmer*, to be directed by Kevin Billington. As Chapman had finished his finals at Bart's and was awaiting his results, it was thought that a summer in the sunshine of Ibiza would be conducive to practical results, and the arrival of Marty Feldman, his wife Loretta, and Tim Brooke-Taylor generated some creative excitement. Frost suddenly decided to fly to Ibiza to see how things were going, and hadn't, so it seems, even established where they were all staying. The first thing Graham Chapman knew about it was a stir in the street while he was having a drink one morning in a sidewalk café, and he saw Frost bearing down on him, brushing off British tourist autograph hounds. Ostensibly his visit was to check up on the progress of the screenplay, but while he was there (including a one-day holiday on the beach) he let it be known that he was intending to produce a comedy show which he hoped to sell to one of the ITV companies. Cleese and Chapman urged him to include Brooke-Taylor in the package, and also Marty Feldman, whose brilliance at comic writing was acknowledged. Feldman and Barry Took had been responsible for *Round the Horne*, one of the funniest of all radio shows. As a result of glandular illness he had developed enormous protruding eyeballs, and looked like a clown who did not have to wear makeup. Frost was persuaded by the others to give Feld-

Peter Cook and John Cleese in the film The Rise and Rise of Michael Rimmer.

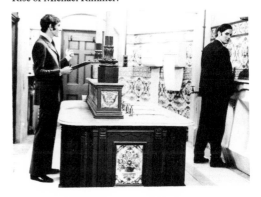

TV TIMES

THE FROST
PHILOSOPHY
pages 16-17

Champion jockey JOSH GIFFORD
looks at the new
NATIONAL HUNT SEASON pages 2-3

COVER :
Tim Brooke-Taylor
John Cleese
Aimi Macdonald
Graham Chapman
Marty Feldman . . .

AT LAST THI
1948 SHOW
Tuesday, 8-45 p.m.

John Cleese, Marty Feldman, Graham Chapman and Tim Brooke-Taylor: At Last The 1948 Show, 1967. Below, joined by the lovely Aimi Macdonald.

man his chance, and then set about selling him to Rediffusion.

The programme was called *At Last the 1948 Show*, and the first one was aired 15 February, 1967. Unlike *The Frost Report* it featured neither Frost, nor a related theme. Holding the show together was Aimi MacDonald, playing a vacuous up-market chorus-girl type, under the impression that the whole thing was built around her. There were two series in 1967, but because of the regional fragmentation of ITV they were not all aired at the same time, many parts of the country not seeing them at all. Yet it was a major step forward on the road to Python, using a multiplicity of television techniques to make its gags, including complicated (to laymen) processes such as inset images and superimposed captions. Some of its sketches had the manic surrealism of the best of Python, piling absurdity on to absurdity in the quest for a comic effect. Old comedy never dies – it merely gets recycled. The celebrated

Judge Not sketch from *Cambridge Circus*, with Cleese as a bewigged barrister getting more and more confused by his own cross-examination, was reprised, among other old favourites. Marty Feldman emerged as a star, in spite of all the doubts about his appearance, and was given a subsequent series of his own, called simply, *Marty*, to which Cleese and Chapman, Palin and Jones contributed material. In the seventies he went to Hollywood where he appeared in a number of films, including a couple directed by Mel Brooks, but he was to die of a heart attack in December 1982, having virtually completed work on location in Mexico for *Yellowbeard*, which Graham Chapman had written in association with Bernard McKenna and Peter Cook.

Meanwhile, Palin and Jones collaborated on a BBC programme with John Bird and John Fortune (who had been John Wood in the Cambridge Footlights) called *A Series of Bird's*, and then appeared with Bill Oddie, Graeme Garden, Jonathan

Terry Jones, Denise Coffey, Michael Palin, David Jason and Eric Idle in Do Not Adjust Your Set. Below, TV Times *cover, 1968.*

Lynn and Dilys Watling in *Twice a Fortnight*, which was produced and directed by another Cambridge man, Tony Palmer. Intended to be a television equivalent of *I'm Sorry, I'll Read That Again*, it was not all that successful. Palmer imported a number of guest rock stars and encouraged the audience to be vociferous, making it difficult sometimes for the comic performers to work properly above the hubbub. Jones and Palin were fortunate in that their material was prefilmed, rather than performed in the studio, and their work achieved a glossy, stylish visual quality that enhanced the hilarity of the subject matter. Their conflicts with Palmer were fewer than those of Oddie and Garden, who nevertheless developed skills which would lead in 1970 to their famous series with Tim Brooke-Taylor, *The Goodies*.

Humphrey Barclay, producer at the BBC of *I'm Sorry, I'll Read That Again* on the radio, had left in 1967 to join Rediffusion, having been invited by Jeremy Isaacs, their programme controller, to mount a comedy show mainly aimed at children, in the same vein. Ignoring the established *At Last the 1948 Show*, Barclay asked Eric Idle and Terry Jones to participate. Terry agreed on condition that his mate, Michael Palin, would also be included. Barclay knew little of him, but quickly appreciated that he would be an appropriate addition, and he also brought in David Jason and Denise Coffey, who were outside the Oxbridge circuit. Barclay called the show *Do Not Adjust Your Set*, a slogan familiar to viewers in the more fault-ridden transmission areas. The first one went out at Christmas 1967, but ironically, owing to some studio mixup the wrong tape was played. It did not fit the special time slot, and had to be curtailed before it had finished, a débâcle which attracted attention as well as rage.

No attempt was made to write directly for children - the tone was bereft of the infuriatingly patronising approach of other areas of juvenile television. Music was provided by the newly-formed Bonzo Dog Doo-Dah Band, a group put together by Neil Innes, a former art student from Goldsmith's College, London. One of their numbers, *Urban Spaceman*, became a hit in its own right and ascended the pop charts. Some of the humour was totally off-the-wall, surreal and absurdist, having an air of fantasy of great appeal to children, but it also caused adults to watch too, although the scheduling slot was before most people had made it home from work. The show was given two seasons - in the winter of 1968 and the spring of 1969 - the second being produced by Ian Davidson instead of Barclay, who by now was at work creating another show, called *We Have Ways of Making You Laugh* for a new company. London Weekend Television had been awarded part of the London franchise in the ITV reshuffle. Barclay's old employers, Rediffusion, were merged with ABC, the then contractors for the Midlands and Northwest, who reformed as Thames, and were awarded the weekday London contract. *We Have Ways of Making You Laugh* was a chat show of no great importance except that it employed the services of Terry Gilliam as a lightning artist, executing his work in split seconds before the cameras. Gilliam, having met John Cleese in New York during *Cambridge Circus* days, had since spent a brief spell in the United States Army (in New Jersey), worked in a Los Angeles advertising agency as an art director, and then had moved to London because his girlfriend of the time, the journalist Glenys Roberts, had become homesick. He had then worked with her on a magazine called *The Londoner*, which was under-capitalised and unsuccessful. Cleese insisted that Barclay meet Gilliam and find work for him. Although a cartoonist himself (he often designed posters for his own programmes), Barclay could not see how he could fit Gilliam's drawings into TV shows. Gilliam persisted and eventually found a rapid way of producing animations, or at least what looked to the untutored eye like animations, but lacked any finesse of movement, figures passing across the screen in a series of jerks. He found that joke sound effects successfully disguised any graphic shortcomings, and helped the comic impact.

There were only two more television milestones to be passed before *Monty Python's Flying Circus* came into being. John Cleese and Graham Chapman wrote

the first programme in a series called *Doctor in the House*, based on the novel by Richard Gordon which in turn had become one of the most successful British comedy films in the mid-fifties. Wisely, they completely revamped the original story and set the pattern for the series, which was continued by Bill Oddie and Graeme Garden (who like Chapman had by now become a qualified doctor). It was one of London Weekend's most successful comedy shows and was followed by such sequels as *Doctor in Charge* and *Doctor at Large*. John Cleese wrote several of them in 1972 and 1973 when he needed some extra money, and one of the shows was based on a hotelier in Torquay he had come across while on location for *Monty Python*, a man of exceptional rudeness and inhospitality. The encounter provided material for a hilarious *Doctor* episode, and Humphrey Barclay pointed out to John that he could build an entire series around such a character, a suggestion which was noted and filed away.

The other show was written by Michael Palin and Terry Jones and was called *The Complete and Utter History of Britain*, the first series of their own. The six programmes took a *1066 and All That* approach to British history, using television techniques, so that Oliver Cromwell appeared to be indulging in a David Frost style interview, and William the Conqueror is interrogated in the changing-rooms after the Battle of Hastings, as though he has just come in from winning against a tough team on their home ground. An actress from Oxford, Diana Quick, was among the cast. The technique in which historical events and characters are represented in present-day idioms was given full rein, and would become a standard element in the Monty Python repertoire, particularly in their films. Alas, in spite of its originality *TCUHB* made little impact and when it concluded no offer of a follow-up was forthcoming, so Jones

Above, *Diana Quick and Terry Jones in 'The Rules of Courtly Love' and Terry Jones and Michael Palin* (below and right) *in Humphrey Barclay's London Weekend Television production of* The Complete and Utter History of Britain, *1969.*

and Palin were free to look around.

Barry Took had now become a comedy producer and general feeder of ideas into the BBC system. It was he who first united the full team. "I had admired Cleese and Chapman, and Palin and Jones. What I had in mind was that Michael Palin and John Cleese should work together – that I thought would be a magic combination. But it was really 'love me, love my dog'. They said they would like the others and Eric Idle. So that was duly arranged. But the BBC was terribly worried about these people. When I met them, and saw how they interplayed – the irritation, the refusal to give an inch, the fact that some came from Oxford and some from Cambridge, I saw that it was absolutely right and to the point. I thought they'll bring different attitudes." Took prevailed on the BBC to take his advice. It was the lighting of the spark that created Monty Python. John Cleese remembers he and Graham Chapman approaching the BBC with an idea for a series after *Do Not Adjust Your Set* with Terry Jones and Michael Palin, and being put in touch with Barry Took. He feels that the inspiration came as much from the future Pythons themselves as from Took.

The six individuals who were to form the Monty Python group in 1969 – Michael Palin, Terry Jones, Terry Gilliam, John Cleese, Graham Chapman and Eric Idle – each talked freely and revealingly about themselves for the purpose of this book. The portraits that follow are mostly based on conversations with each Python during the winter and spring of 1983. Occasional discrepancies of recollection between one individual and another have been retained. How a man remembers his past says much about him – the Pythons have managed to merge and homogenise their talents in their joint work with extraordinary skill, yet retain distinctive, disparate personalities of their own. They have a number of common rules for their collective conduct – resistance to being leaned on, for instance, and an unusually forceful protective instinct where their material is concerned. While they are flexible and critical among themselves, outsiders who tamper are likely to find a singular lack of co-operation.

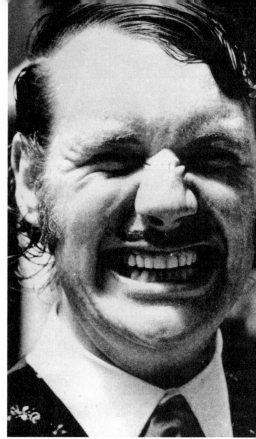

MICHAEL

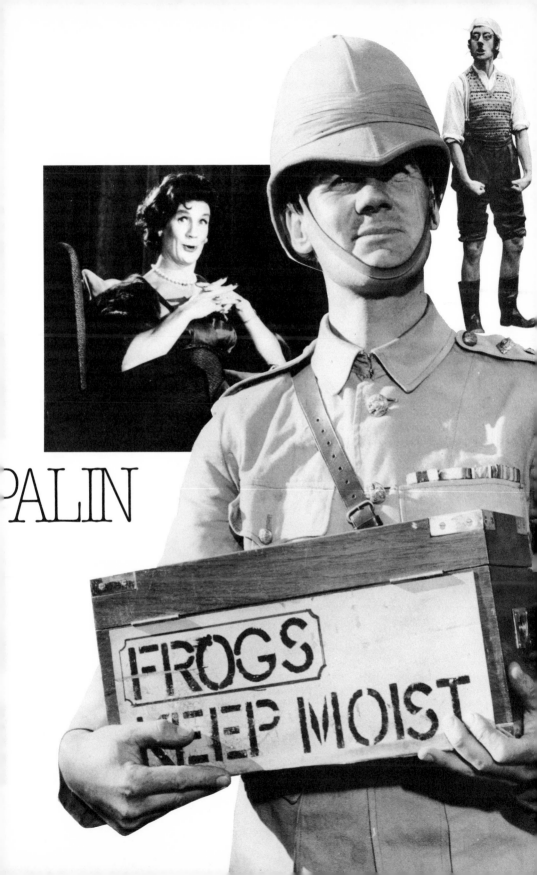

PALIN

FROGS KEEP MOIST

1956

Michael Palin, back row right,
as scorer for the
Birkdale Preparatory School XI, 1956.

BY A MATTER OF weeks Michael Palin is the youngest of the Pythons, having been born on 5 May, 1943. (The closest of his colleagues in age is Eric Idle who entered the world on 29 March of that year.) He's a Yorkshireman, from Sheffield, which may explain why he feels that people should not live in Surrey. His father spent most of his working life in the engineering offices of Edgar Allen and Company, one of the steel firms in that city. Michael was the second of the Palins' two children, the first being a daughter, Angela, born nine years earlier. His childhood was spent happily in a large, stone-built late Victorian house at Ranmoor, near the southern slopes of the Pennines.

"My father was quite strict. He was insistent on things like mealtimes – lunch had to be exactly at ten-past-one, supper at exactly twenty-past-seven. He didn't like me bringing friends home in the evening, which was quite hard because I was fairly gregarious. I used to spend a great deal of time next door with a chap called Graham Stuart-Harris who still lives in Sheffield – his father was a doctor and they had a far more easy-going regime in their house. We had a very regular existence – two weeks holiday in the summer where we went to one of two places, either Sheringham in Norfolk or Southwold in Suffolk. Creature of habit my father was. The house was in the better part of Sheffield, but it was rented, it wasn't owned. My father didn't really earn a great deal of money. I was surprised after he died and I found out how much he had been earning when he sent me away to public school. It must have cost about a third of his income. What I saw as parsimony was really the result of necessity – we couldn't afford exotic holidays. I remember we got our television eight or nine years after the Stewart-Harrises, for instance."

His father sent him to Shrewsbury, having been educated there himself. It was the school at which the founding fathers of *Private Eye*, the satirical fortnightly started in 1962, had received their education a few years earlier, and Michael remembers being shown copies of *Mesopotamia*, its Oxford precursor, by a history master. "It was certainly a cut above *The Salopian*, our school magazine to which I contributed the occasional match report. There was a lot of sport at school. I remember being permanently cold and short of breath, and carrying vast amounts of books from our house to the main school buildings, taking care not to walk over certain parts of the grounds you couldn't step on until you had been there for four years. Shrewsbury was a great home for elaborate practical jokes. Even the masters would play practical jokes on each other. Our house was a very happy one, largely due to a wonderful housemaster who was very silly, full of jokes. He kept us full of laughter, and enabled us to cope with the awful food and waking up in winter with six inches of snow on our beds."

Michael Palin's father, having succeeded in getting him into his old school, would have rather liked him to go on to his old college, Clare, at Cambridge, but it was to Oxford instead that the youth gravitated.

"I wasn't scholarship material, but the school thought that I should have a go, since it would help me get a place. I went up to Oxford for the Magdalen and Worcester exams, and they gave me some of the most embarrassing moments of my life. The interviewer at Worcester, particularly. I wanted to read English, and I had mugged up on Graham Greene, still one of my favourite authors. They asked what authors I read, and when I said Greene, they said no, no, authors on the syllabus. It was then that I realised English at Oxford stopped in 1900. So I tried to get out of it by saying I liked poetry. They asked me, whose poetry? You know how it is when you are on the run – your mind seizes up. I couldn't think of anyone. After a long pause I said 'Wordsworth!' The man must have scented blood, because he said 'Name six of his poems!' After another forty seconds I said 'Michael', then eventually I muttered 'Daffodils'. Well that was Worcester. And then for the Magdalen exam I can remember getting a general paper which had a quote on it, 'A house is a machine for living in – Le Corbusier. Discuss.' And I can remember starting 'Of course this was all right when Le Corbusier lived in the sixteenth century, but now things are very different!' In the end I got in to Brasenose, I'm not sure why! And I read history, which was safer."

In his latter days at Shrewsbury he had begun to write what he describes as self-conscious humorous pieces, and had begun to develop a talent for it, abetted by the housemaster who refused to take things seriously. After gaining his place at Oxford he left school with two terms to spare, and filled in the months before going up working in the publicity department of his father's firm, Edgar Allen's, in Sheffield where he wrote a few facetious pieces for the works magazine. "I just mucked around in Sheffield while I was waiting for Oxford – I didn't do anything exotic like crossing the Sahara. It was a very happy time. I joined a local dramatic group, the Brightside and Carbrook Co-operative Society Players. We did heavy acting, a play called *The Woodcarver* about a realist carving of a statue of Christ for instance, and I remember doing a love scene on a couch with a lady who was seven months pregnant. My father didn't want me to be an actor, apart from very

small parts in school plays. I think he thought it would interfere with my work. My sister joined a professional repertory company, and I know he would have preferred her to be a secretary. But he didn't mind me acting after I had left school because I had got my place at Oxford.

"Oxford was a revelation. There was so much freedom, so many things to do. I started off going in for sport, but then I realised how miserable it was, playing football in the cold, so after a few weeks I faded out. I made friends with Robert Hewison, who I suppose after Graham Stuart-Harris, my childhood friend, influenced me more than anyone else. He was a sort of urbane, smooth sophisticate from London and a bit of a joker, rather good at telling stories, and putting on funny voices, and I could see there was going to be trouble there, opposition. So if you can't beat 'em, join 'em. Robert and I became very good friends, and it was an opening for me into a quite different world. He was the driving force behind getting me to join OUDS and to start writing down the little comedy improvis-

ations we used to do up in his room."

Hewison instilled a great sense of confidence in the lad from the provinces, and made the previously unattainable ambition of joining the likes of Spike Milligan, Michael Bentine, Eric Sykes as comedy writers a credible possibility. Both of them had become authorities on radio and television comedy, and had listened to the great shows all through their adolescence. They wrote material for college revue clubs and bemoaned the absence of an organisation as advanced as the Cambridge Footlights. "Robert was ambitious, and whereas my friends tended to be unfashionable, he used to get to know those who were successful. That's how I met Terry Jones, who was a quite well-known Oxford figure. He used to have an amazing dark-brown, hairy check coat, I remember, and he was tanned and dark, not pink-cheeked like I was. He had his own set-up at Teddy Hall, was much involved in the ETC plays that Michael Rudman did, and Brecht. Brecht was the big thing then, and Terry was definitely in the senior league. The first time we wrote together was for a show in a mar-

quee called *Loitering Within Tent*."

The other partnership that Robert Hewison was instrumental in fostering was that with Michael Palin's future wife, Helen. "I'd met her on a holiday when I was quite young, about sixteen – it was a teenage holiday romance – and then I didn't see her for a long time. She lived in Cambridgeshire. She wrote me a note saying that she had heard that I had got into Oxford, and that they must have lowered the standards – something sarcastic like that – and that was all. Then Robert said that I must meet his girlfriend, called Piglet, who was in London at a teachers' training college, and it turned out to be the one at which Helen was also studying. So the girls came up to Oxford together. We were married in 1966, a year after I had left the university."

In his second year at Oxford he concentrated more on straight acting, appearing in the ETC production of Harold Pinter's

Left, The Woodcarver *performed by the Brightside and Carbrook Co-operative Players, 1962, Michael Palin at right.* Below, Hang Down Your Head And Die, *the Oxford ETC attack on capital punishment, 1964, with Michael Palin centre.*

The Birthday Party, and also attempting to catch up on his studies which had sagged. The high point of the year was Braham Murray's *Hang Down Your Head and Die*, the ETC revue about capital punishment, which after much surgery and sweat, opened in triumph and transferred to the West End for a limited run. "That was the first time that I felt there was a chance that after Oxford I could earn my living as an actor or a writer, or both."

During the summer of that year, 1964, Palin went to Edinburgh and appeared with Terry Jones in *The Oxford Revue*, with Nigel Pegram, Douglas Fisher and Annabel Leventon. The *Monty Python* style of comedy had antecedents in that show, then much under the influence of *Beyond the Fringe*. It was the show with the famous custard pie lecture that was passed on to *Cambridge Circus*. It was also Terry Jones' farewell to Oxford, but Michael Palin still had another year, which culminated in *The Oxford Line*, a show which advanced the surreal craziness even further.

In London Terry Jones had enlisted Palin's help in writing the abortive musical for Willie Donaldson on the subject of love, but it had the effect of prolonging their writing collaboration beyond the university. Then as Terry J. joined the BBC, Michael Palin, now a graduate, facing the fact that a regular job was necessary, landed an assignment with TWW, the doomed Bristol ITV contractor which was shortly to have its franchise wiped out when renewal time came round. His healthy, youthful, clean-cut appearance succeeded in securing for him the post of anchorman on a teenage pop programme called *Now*, transmitted to Wales and parts of the West of England for six months. The show was too cheaply put together to make television history, but apart from providing useful income, which deterred Michael Palin from becoming a nine-to-five copywriter in an advertising agency, it gave him very useful experience in facing live cameras.

Meanwhile, he and Terry Jones had been doing cabaret spots in places such as the Rehearsal Club, and their work had attracted the interest of David Frost, who

AUDIENCE

Monday 6 November

DO NOT ADJUST YOUR SET

The Fairly Pointless Show

ADMIT ONE

you to
DAVID
and th

was scouting for writers to subscribe to his new BBC series *The Frost Report*. It turned out to be the first gathering of the future Pythons, all of whom except Terry Gilliam were drafted in to form the scripting team. It also cemented the writing partnership of Jones and Palin, which developed further when they worked together on *A Series of Bird's*, the six-episode comedy series starring John Bird and John Fortune, both from Cambridge, and *Twice a Fortnight*, another show dominated by ex-Footlights such as Bill Oddie, Jonathan Lynn and Graeme Garden, and produced by Tony Palmer. Terry Jones, invited by Humphrey Barclay to contribute to *Do Not Adjust Your Set*, got him to agree with the proviso that Michael Palin also be brought in, a request readily granted, and the two of them, with Eric Idle, David Jason and Denise Coffey formed a successful comedy team. Barclay went on to produce a joke history series called *The Complete and Utter History of*

SION LONDON invites

DO NOT ADJUST YOUR SET

INSTRUCTIONS FOR AUDIENCE

1. Do not adjust your parents.
2. Place them tidily in front of the Television Set.
3. Do not play with them.
4. Give them a bone to chew and come to Rediffusion Television Studios, Empire Way, Wembley on Monday, November 6th, 1967. (8.30 - 9.15 p.m. Doors open 8.00 - 8.15 p.m.)
5. Laugh.

This ticket admits ONE PERSON (provided he or she is 10 or over)

ENISE COFFEY·ERIC IDLE
TERRY JONES·MIKE PALIN
ZO DOG DOO-DAH BAND

Above, admission ticket for a recording of 'The Fairly Pointless Show', otherwise known as 'Do Not Adjust Your Set'. Right, *Michael Palin in a sketch with Ronnie Corbett for* Frost on Sunday.

Britain, which Palin and Jones wrote entirely themselves as well as performing in, but although the technique of presenting historical events and personalities in a modern manner at that time seemed refreshingly original and often ingenious, poor scheduling led to moderate ratings. Luckily, the call came from the BBC, in the guise of Barry Took, shortly afterwards to meet and arrange for the series that would become *Monty Python's Flying Circus*.

"We all submerged our idiosyncrasies during the first series, and were rather polite to one another," Palin recalls. He is by nature more reflective and less excitable than Terry Jones, and thus usually avoided locking horns with the devastatingly candid John Cleese. The Jones-

Palin axis, much influenced by Spike Milligan's manic series *Q5*, which had torn apart the rules of television comedy, were responsible for the fragmented structure of the shows, and for inserting their wild flights of visual imagination. Jones and Palin favoured ghastly locations, ludicrously uncomfortable costumes and much hardship and privation to create funny filmed inserts, never minding how much pain and ridicule they would endure for the sake of the show. They found an unexpected ally in Terry Gilliam, who apart from possessing a weird visual sense very much in tune with their own fantasies, also had a regard for the remote past, an obsession for ancient times corresponding to Terry Jones' fascination for Chaucer and Michael Palin's love of the Arthurian legend.

Michael's wish to make a film about King Arthur inspired the first true Monty Python film, *Monty Python and the Holy Grail*. In the original outline the Holy Grail was going to be found in Harrod's department store and there was to be much more confusion between the past and the present, but after the screenplay had emerged from many heavy sessions with all six Pythons, the only modern intrusion, apart from the verbal ones, was the police squad car that arrives at the end to arrest certain members of the cast. The remote Scottish locations, however, were entirely due to the insistence of Jones and Palin.

"There was and is a straight Oxford–Cambridge split. Oxford people can put up with far more discomfort. The Cambridge people cannot intellectually justify why they should be so uncomfortable when they could be just as funny in the studio. Terry and I always felt that we needed something extra, perhaps due to some deep-seated inadequacy in ourselves. It's always the way it was. I used sometimes to get very cross privately at home that everyone wasn't pulling their weight when things like finishing off a record, or going to see a bit of dubbing came along, things that didn't need everybody. The only two who could ever be contacted were Terry Jones and me because we were at home. But in a way it's got a way of working itself out. It would be absolutely

Michael Palin and Terry Jones attempt to hypnotise a brick.

disastrous if we were all the same, and did the same amount of work and never grumbled. It would have been awful. The centrifugal feeling that Python has is terribly important. It might have now gone too far – everyone having gone off to areas of their own. There are so many excuses not to do any more Python.

"I would like us to do another film together – I think that we could make it fresh. As performers we can still enjoy ourselves a great deal, and I think that we can produce work that is better than anything we have ever done before. After doing *The Meaning of Life* I really think it can be. But we won't be rushing into it."

Palin has managed to achieve substantial successes away from the group, both in partnership with Terry Jones, and in his own right. In 1973 together they wrote a television play called *Secrets* which was transmitted in a BBC drama series under the heading *Black and Blue*. Warren Mitchell played the lead in a black comedy about a chocolate factory where some men who have fallen in a mixing vat end up as fillings for confectionery. After favourable marketing reports from areas where the chocolates have been sent they attempt to reproduce the effect with animal meat, but the results are not the same so the factory recruited human volunteers.

Something of this dark imagination was incorporated in a book he and Terry Jones produced in 1974 called *Bert Fegg's Nasty Book for Boys and Girls* (in the United States it became *Dr Fegg's Nasty Book of Knowledge*) which contained such items as "The Famous Five Go Pillaging" and "Across the Andes by Frog".

In 1975 he played in a film of *Three Men in a Boat*, made for BBC television by Stephen Frears. The other upriver rowers in Jerome K. Jerome's classic account of a Thames holiday were Tim Curry and Stephen Moore. Another BBC director, Terry Hughes, wanted the Jones–Palin team to make a series, and they came up with a script for a pilot, called *Tomkinson's Schooldays*. The intention was to take a familiar genre of Victorian and Edwardian children's literature, the public school

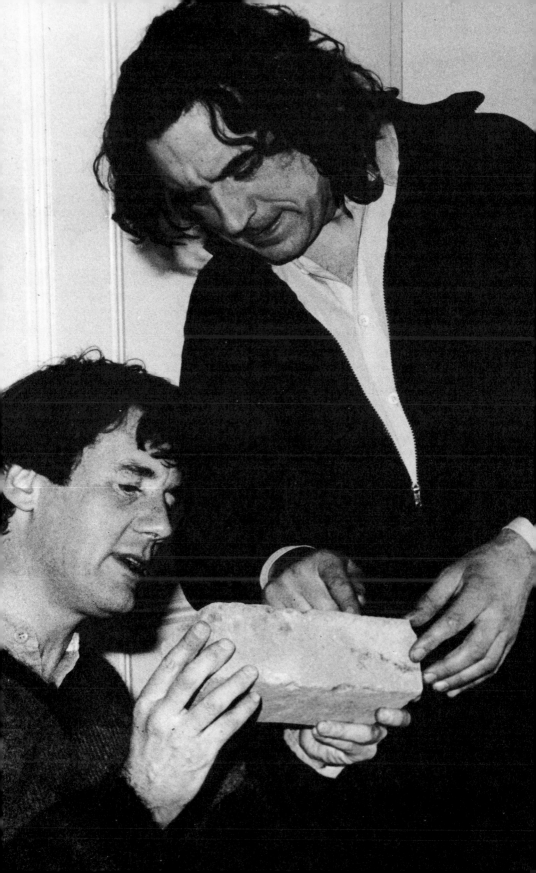

story, and to make it the basis of an outrageous spoof.

The programme was made entirely on film, which meant that it could be given a distinctive look and strong production values. A successful reception for the one-off programme led to the commissioning of a series under the heading *Ripping Yarns*. Each one was different in mood and subject, the only unifying feature being the suggestion that their provenance was juvenile fiction of yesteryear. They included *Escape from Stalag 112B*, *Murder at Moorstones Manor*, *Across the Andes by Frog* (again) and in the second series *Roger of the Raj* and *Winfrey's Last Stand*. Each was a complete filmed story and there were nine altogether, three of which were directed by Terry Hughes, the rest by Jim Franklin and Alan J.W. Bell. Even though they were hilarious send-ups of the various genres, the respect for the past which Palin and Jones have was sufficient to ensure that the background atmosphere was authentic, and its verisimilitude heightened the comedy.

Terry Gilliam asked Michael Palin to play his Candide-like hero in the film *Jabberwocky*, in which as an innocent cooper's apprentice he finds himself mistaken for a prince and called upon to rid the kingdom of a fearsome monster that has menaced the population for far too long. Gilliam's view of the period required the cast to smear themselves with mud and pick their way through slime and garbage, an ordeal which failed to diminish Michael Palin's cheerful enthusiasm. He was to collaborate again with Gilliam on the screenplay of *Time Bandits*, although his appearance in that film was in a minor role as one of a pair of lovers who seem to have been conducting an affair through many historical eras.

In 1980 the BBC gave him an opportunity to indulge one of his special pleasures – trains. He was asked to make a documentary in their series *Great Railway Journeys of the World*, and while other notables such as Michael Frayn and Ludovic Kennedy were travelling many thousands of miles across the United States or Australia, he was quite happy to make a simple journey to the West Coast of Scotland, a country for which he feels a particular affection. The programme was as revealing of the gentle nature of Michael Palin's personality as an in-depth interview, and demonstrated his almost Betjemanesque sensitivity for landscape and the smooth motion of wheel upon rail.

His ambitions with regard to film-making have increased, and in 1982 he wrote, co-produced and starred in a film backed by George Harrison and Denis O'Brien called *The Missionary*. He played an exile returning to England after years of proselytising in the African bush, coming back to an Edwardian England steeped in hypocrisy and social prejudice. Urged by his bishop to establish a refuge for fallen women in London's East End, he is seduced by the nymphomaniac wife of a bellicose peer and shamelessly uses her money for his purpose, which gets ever more complicated. The film was photographed with great care and attention to compositions, and looks magnificent. (The director was Richard Loncraine who had earlier been an artist – the kinetic sculptures in John Schlesinger's *Sunday Bloody Sunday* were his.) An ample budget enabled a strong cast to be assembled which included Denholm Elliott as the bishop, Trevor Howard as the rich peer, and Maggie Smith his voracious wife, David Suchet a murderous gillie and Phoebe Nicholls as our hero's dim-witted fiancee who has passionately filed his love letters in an unfathomably complex system for seven years without reading them and believes fallen women to be women who have hurt their knees. The performance that shone most was that of Michael Hordern as an aged butler, incapable of remembering what he is doing, where he is going or indeed in which room he is, in the peer's vast stately home.

There were lessons to be learnt from *The Missionary* – for instance, the fact that it had a superabundance of good ideas, each of which were strong enough to cancel out the effects of the others. Audiences expecting an extended *Ripping Yarn* were disappointed; the laughs were a great deal more subtle and intermittent. Palin was able to extend his acting range more effec-

Above, *A cheeky view of Michael Palin in* Jabberwocky *directed by Terry Gilliam*. Below, *Palin as* The Missionary *with three fallen women*.

54

tively than any of the other Pythons, and is perhaps the only one of them who could play a straight role without the shadow of Python interfering. "He's the only actor among us," says Terry Gilliam, "the rest of us are just caricaturists." Gilliam hopes to cast him as a villain in his new film which is scripted by Tom Stoppard.

Michael Palin lives in Oak Village, a small enclave of Victorian houses south of Hampstead Heath. His London house is modest, small in scale, but attractively furnished and decorated. He has converted the loft into his study, a studio room with plenty of light, a tiny terrace and plenty of built-in furniture. He has also bought a similar nearby house which backs on to the same internal courtyard, with the intention of expanding available space. The Palins have three children, two sons and a daughter, and intend to provide nearby separate quarters for them, so that he can work in his rooftop eyrie undisturbed except for the telephone and the occasional buzz of aircraft as as they bank into their final approach for Heathrow Airport. He enjoys being at home and being a family man. "I'm a bit of an armchair traveller, although I love going to exotic places. I've just taken the family to Kenya and Australia, but on the whole I don't have many holidays. I'd like to organise a project where I could go to all the places I dreamed about when I was a child. That's why *Great Railway Journeys* was such a good idea." He is neat, files his papers carefully, and maintains copious notes on his life as it goes along. During the filming of *The Missionary* he would spend much time in his trailer writing up his journal. Eventually a definitive Palin autobiography must emerge, if he can bring himself to the Herculean task of editing it down.

Just as Terry Jones has pursued romanticism by investing money in projects such as *Vole*, an ecology magazine which eventually failed, and a brewery that produced real ale, Michael Palin has a small publishing imprint called Signford which has produced slender books of illustration by Chris Orr, notes on Ruskin, and verse by Alfred Levinson, in association with Robert Hewison. The parent company is the Gumby Corporation, taking its name from the grotesque booted, pullovered figure invented by Palin for the Python shows. It is the sort of publishing that enables worthwhile work that might otherwise go unseen to get some sort of exposure. He has also written, as has Terry Jones, stories directly for children, although the juvenile book market is one of the highest risk areas in publishing.

He is working on another film of his own, but after *The Meaning of Life* and *The Missionary*, both of which required extensive promotional tours, resolves to take things easy for a while. "I like to wait for something to happen. It usually does."

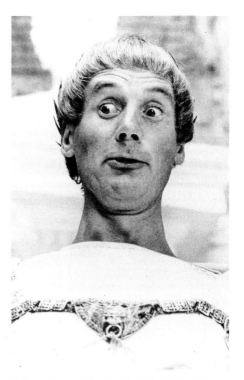

Left, *as Pontius Pilate in* The Life of Brian. *Right, Country-lover Palin opens the City Farm in the heart of Camden, 1982.*

TERRY
JONES

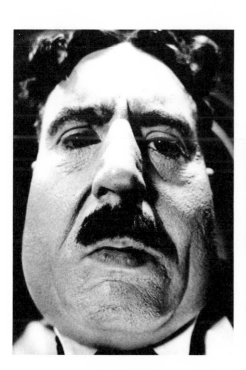

*Terry Jones at Guildford Royal Grammar School
captains the 1st XV, 1960.*

THAT THE PYTHONS can still come together and perform is as much due to the energy and enthusiasm of Terry Jones as any other factor – he is the one who has shouldered the Python torch and held it aloft and aflame. "It's the Welsh blood, you see," he says, "we're all so terribly enthusiastic! In a Welsh accent, if you make a suggestion you get excited at the end of a sentence, but if you make a suggestion in a Surrey accent you go down at the end of the sentence, and it comes out hard, as though you're laying down the law. This fact came to me only about five or six years ago when I realised that people sometimes find me hard to take – even my wife has said I can be very dominating."

He was born in North Wales on 1 February, 1942, in the pleasant resort of Colwyn Bay, which he now regards as a Liverpool suburb. His father was a Denbigh native, but his mother came from Bolton, Lancashire. "My father always wanted to be a carpenter, but he was a bank clerk all his life, one of the great wastes – it was regarded as a good steady job during the depression. When he eventually retired he became a changed man and started living for the first time." In fact, he had a break from Barclays Bank during the war years when he served in the Royal Air Force in Calcutta. At the end of the war, the family, including Terry's brother Nigel, who was two years older than him, moved south to Claygate, Surrey. "It scarred me for life, and I spent the next fifteen years going around saying I was Welsh, hating this place we had moved to in commuter Surrey, away from Colwyn Bay with its beach and Fairy Glen and Iris Park. We lived in a little semi-detached house, and as I was five I went to the local Church of England primary school. From about the age of six I was going to be a poet – my first poem was called 'Prairie Fires' if I remember right. I never read anything then. I went on to the Royal Grammar School at Guildford."

His schoolboy keenness propelled him into leading the rugby team and the Corps, and he had what he describes as a reputation for being a goody-goody. "Any work I was given I automatically did. I suppose that I was a bit of a swot, although I didn't mean to be." Unfortunately acting was not on the school curriculum. "The headmaster felt that actors were by definition homosexuals and communists. I can remember him giving us a lecture on homosexuality in which he said the sure sign of one was green suede shoes. I've never worn them since!"

English was the subject in which he shone, and he rapidly discovered an aversion to mathematics as well as a distinct lack of scientific skill. Ironically he nearly failed his A-level English by failing to read the instruction and completing four essays on Shakespeare when only two were required and marked, thus leaving no time to do the rest of the paper. He stayed on for a third year in the Sixth Form and was turned down by a succession of universities – Exeter, Bristol, London and Manchester. He then went to Cambridge for an interview at Gonville and Caius College, where he was described as a mixture of simplicity and sophistication and invited to take their entrance examination. He also took the exam for a place at St Edmund Hall, Oxford. "I didn't really want to go to Teddy Hall. I didn't want to do Latin and Anglo-Saxon. Caius would have been very exciting, where my tutor would have been Donald Davie who contributed poetry to the *New Statesman*. But I was offered a place at Teddy Hall, and then, a week after I had accepted I was offered one at Caius. My school put pressure on me not to change. So I went to Oxford!"

But for that accident of timing, with one letter preceding another in the mail, the formation of the Monty Python team might not have happened. Terry Jones believes that had he gone to Cambridge he would have stayed firmly in the arms of academe, steering clear of the Footlights, which to him seemed much to organised. He entered Oxford in October 1961. "I was very impressed by the corduroy suits, a sign of rebellion in those days. I was very intimidated by the place in my first year, and it took me three years to find out that it wasn't quite as impressive as I thought it was going to be." While not entirely relishing the linguistic struggle to decipher *Beowulf*, he enjoyed

the opportunities to get to grips with Milton, and was particularly happy in Middle English, where he found his metier. "Even at school I'd had quite a strong pull towards Chaucer – I felt that he was a good guy, and my admiration for him has been growing ever since.

"I got into the theatre scene via the college show, really. Even at school we had done a little, such as end of term revues – I remember getting all the prefects doing a chicken chorus. But at Teddy Hall there was a sudden intake of thespians. We had Michael Rudman that year reading English and he quickly took over the college drama society. I was in his first production. I then found myself doing little funny roles. In my second year I did a revue. Ian Davidson, Doug Fisher and Robin Grove-White had done one the year before with Paul McDowell and were going up to Edinburgh with it, but Paul

McDowell suddenly had a hit song, *You're Driving Me Crazy* which he recorded with The Temperance Seven, which took up all of his time and so I was asked to go instead. It was pretty successful that year and came down to London, first at the LAMDA theatre, then at the Phoenix. It was called **** (four asterisks). When I went back for my third year I had a certain cachet because I had been on the West End stage, and suddenly everybody wanted me to be in their production. I eventually decided to do this thing with Braham Murray for the Experimental Theatre Club, called *Hang Down Your Head and Die* about capital punishment. We spent two terms preparing – it was going to be total theatre and everybody was going to write it. Michael Palin was in it as well. I had met him just a bit before. We were appalled at the final script that was produced – it was much

Left, *School Captain, Terry Jones, conducts a prefects' room jape.* Above, *Ian Davidson and Terry Jones in* The Good Woman of Seuzan, *Oxford 1962.*

too long and we were all panicking. I remember - the first time I wrote with Mike - he and Robert Hewison and I stayed up all one night and went through the show and organised it and went to Braham but didn't meet with much approval at that stage. How it got on I don't know, but we did it."

Like John Cleese, Terry Jones was heavily influenced by *The Goon Show* on the radio. He can even remember as a child listening to *ITMA*. "I was also keen on *Up the Pole* with Jewel and Warris, and *Much-Binding-in-the-Marsh*. I've always been a sparse reader, though. I used to go to the movies. I remember seeing Danny Kaye pulling faces and deciding that I could do that, and I wanted to be a film star. That is - apart from a short period, after which I thought I might like to be a classical composer - for about three days. I didn't watch television very much but I

remember greatly enjoying Michael Bentine's *It's a Square World* because he was using the medium to produce visual humour. But I suppose it was Jacques Tati who really got me going on that. At Oxford I was never particularly into films - I was too busy with other things. I worked on *Isis*, the undergraduate magazine, designing it, and I rather envied Cambridge's expertise in that area. I was laying-out *Isis* in the morning, rehearsing some play in the afternoon, and in the evenings I usually did a bit of reading - ah, typical Oxford days!"

Financially Terry Jones was hard-up during his university years. His means-tested grant depended on a top-up from his parents who were unable to afford it. In vacations he worked at a variety of odd jobs, including collecting household refuse for his local authority, the Esher Urban District Council. "It was a wonderful atmosphere – there was a tremendous *esprit de corps* among the dustmen. You could tell what day of the week it was by what road you were in, and the time of day by where you were in that road. I came away with a new perception. I started looking at houses in a new way. Normally you look at the front door. But after two weeks of dustbins I was looking for the side door. The whole house was orientated around the dustbin."

He had always thought that he would end up as an academic, pursuing English studies. "I was sitting in the Bodleian Library one day, reading what somebody had written about what somebody else had written about what somebody else had written about what Milton wrote. And I was getting very indignant about this thing, feeling very strongly about it, and I thought 'What on earth am I doing?' I resolved that I might enjoy doing that later on in life, but for the next ten years or so I'd prefer to write the original thing in the first place, rather than writing about what somebody else had written."

After *Hang Down Your Head* only one term was left at Oxford, and after his finals in which he managed a second-class degree he went up to Edinburgh with the Oxford Theatre Group to do the revue with Michael Palin, Doug Fisher, Nigel Pegram and Annabel Leventon. "We were very excited about it because we felt that it was a break from tradition. The four asterisks revue had been much in the mould of *Beyond the Fringe*, all based on social manners. But The Oxford Revue was more off-the-wall, more fantastic. We did some very odd bits. We all sang a song about British nosh, and Michael had a song about having a long-range telescope. It got a terrific response. David Frost came round, but alas, we ended up with it in the Establishment Club, which had become very seedy by then. We often outnumbered the audience, which was strange because in Edinburgh we had played to packed houses. And of course, the most famous number in it was the custard pie sketch which we gave to *Cambridge Circus*.

"I remember meeting John Cleese then. He really wasn't that much different from now. I remember having dinner with him in the Angus Steak House in Leicester Square and being very impressed by the amount of steak that he could put away. Michael White invited us to a party with the Cambridge lot. Anyway, that started off my first year out of Oxford."

Although broke, Terry Jones preferred to live in a cheap room in Earls Court than at home in Claygate. Willie Donaldson put up a small sum of money as a commission for him to write his proposed show about sex, in spite of his lack of experience in that area. For weeks Terry Jones was combing libraries looking for references to the history of lovemaking, to be turned

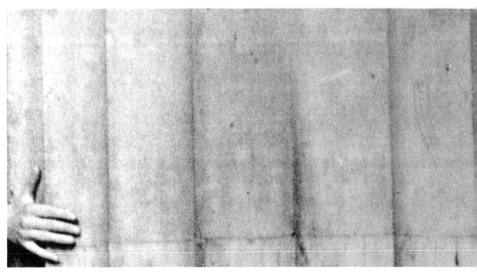

into a musical on the lines of *Hang Down Your Head and Die*. Michael Palin, a year behind him at Oxford, later joined in the stillborn project. He also earned a small sum in collaboration with Miles Kington on a TV programme for Rediffusion which was never produced.

"I had a Thai girlfriend who was still up at Oxford and she was giving me rather a hard time, and I'd come to the end of the Rediffusion thing and didn't have any other work. I had a particularly bad phone call from her and I felt I had to go up and see her or else see the end of the relationship, and at that time I was living in Lambeth and I remember walking across Lambeth Bridge and I got halfway over and I thought 'Sod it!' – no, no, I wasn't thinking of committing suicide! I was overwhelmed by the symbolism of crossing bridges, and I thought – 'This is no good, Oxford's a dead end and I'm not going to get anywhere.' So I turned round and went back again and started phoning up people to get a job – it had not occurred to me before to try and get a job, and I nearly became a copywriter for Anglia Television. And then I suddenly got a phone call from Frank Muir's secretary asking me to go and meet him. He offered me a job at £20 a week at the BBC in Light Entertainment, to be a script editor officially, but to hang around and keep an eye on television and go to meetings and listen. I remember sitting in on discus-

Above, *Terry Jones on cabaret tour in Torquay, 1963*. Left, *Edinburgh 1964 for the Oxford Theatre group revue*.

sions on *The Frost Report*, and whether they should go ahead with it or not, with people saying 'Well, David Frost is a bit past it, isn't he?' It was a very interesting time – I had an office and a desk with four telephones on it. Occasionally I had stabs at writing sketches that never quite made it. But eventually I contributed a joke to Ken Dodd – it was the year Ken Dodd made it – and in the Review of the Year they mentioned it with *my* joke, about a policeman's walking race. Actually, it was Miles's joke."

After six months Muir sent him on a BBC director's course which he was unable to finish because he got peritonitis. After a frustrating period as a production assistant, a dogsbody job for which he felt no aptitude, he became attached to Rowan Ayres who was producing a programme to round off each evening on BBC2, called *Late Night Line-Up.* "He took me on as a jokesmith to add a humour element, particularly the Friday night one, and I wrote with Michael Palin, Barry Cryer and Robert Hewison. I didn't do the performing – they did it. It went terribly well for the first few weeks until Denis Tuohy, the presenter, came back from the States, and I think he felt that it all had been done behind his back. We noticed that people weren't laughing in the control room anymore. We lasted a little longer, contributing odd funny lines, but eventually left. Mike and I then began writing for *The Frost Report,* particularly visual jokes, our first taste of actual filming."

During his time at the BBC he met Alison, then newly graduated from Oxford and working as a technician in the Botany Department of London University. They moved in together and eventually bought a three-storeyed Victorian house in Grove Park on the heights between Camberwell and Dulwich. They married in 1970 and still live there. At Oxford they never met, but Alison recalls Terry and Michael Palin doing a cabaret at Lady Margaret Hall, her college, and being sick in the middle of the performance. "I do remember someone being ushered out in the middle of one of my sketches," says Terry. "I didn't know it was my future wife and the mother of my children!" Since then she has pursued a successful career well-distanced from show-business, as a biochemist specialising in photosynthesis at Imperial College, London.

The Jones household is a friendly, slightly frenetic place. The top floor is Terry's study, two rooms converted to one, with a view to the north over the rooftops to the high-rise buildings of the City and the dome of St Paul's. "We've been here since 1969. Sometimes we think we should have moved, to the depths of the country perhaps, but we like it here. It seems to get better all the time – we have a real neighbourhood now in Grove Park. There's a noticeboard where people can advertise anything they want on the corner, and every year they put on a pantomime, ostensibly for the children's benefit."

His path towards the Pythons took him via the show Humphrey Barclay invited him to write for Rediffusion, *Do Not Adjust Your Set,* which he agreed to do on condition that Michael Palin be brought into it as well, and which Eric Idle also joined. It was followed by other shows such as *Broaden Your Mind* and *Marty* for the BBC which also involved John Cleese and Graham Chapman. "In the last series of *Do Not Adjust Your Set* a chap named Terry Gilliam had been hanging round, and had done a couple of animations. Eric was rather keen that he be involved. Michael and I meanwhile did a series for London Weekend, *The Complete and Utter History of Britain.* Then Barry Took suggested we all link up and do something for BBC. We were given thirteen programmes. I remember thinking at the time that there was no question it wasn't going to be the funniest show around, because John and Graham were writing wonderful material, and we thought we could write very funny material, too, of a different kind – John and Graham were very verbal and we were a bit wackier and visual. In those days it was still Hugh Greene's time as Director-General, and the fact that they could say 'All right, thirteen shows, then!' without a pilot or anything, shows the great confidence the BBC had then, and the freedom the individual producers had. I remember being very keen to get a distinctive format for the show. Then Spike Milligan had his series Q5. Suddenly I realised we had all been writing cliches!"

Terry Jones was fascinated by the technical aspects of constructing the programmes, particularly the filmed inserts, and fought hard to overcome the reluctance of their director, Ian McNaughton, to allow him in on the editing. Eventually, when confidence was established, he not only put scenes together but directed location sequences, being particularly fond of remote, rain-soaked parts of Britain which had not been seen much on television. He and Terry Gilliam were clearly

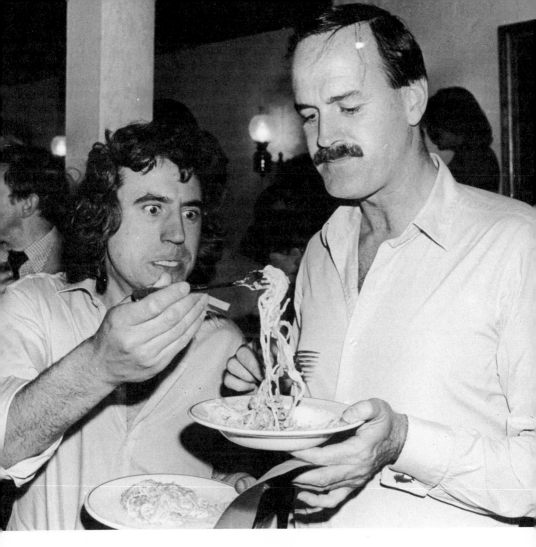

The Pythons always enjoy dining together. Terry Jones appears to have found something on John Cleese's plate.

the most visually conscious members of the team and also possessed a tolerable knowledge of film grammar. After the hastily made *And Now for Something Completely Different* film, which had re-hashed much of the television material, and had been subjected to heavy interference from Victor Lownes, the producer, the Pythons were anxious to retain control of their next film project, *Monty Python and the Holy Grail* and the two Terrys were appointed co-directors. "I really agree very easily about things – I especially did then. We had very similar ideas. I enjoyed it, but I think Terry found it a frustrating experience. The filming was a nightmare. Everybody was underpaid, including us, and doing it half for love. I felt badly about that because at

least we had a percentage, whereas the technicians were not only underpaid but had no share. We had this loony schedule – scenes that should take a week were shot in a day. The sequence with the Knights who say 'Ni!', for instance, which is nearly ten minutes of cut film – done in a day!"

One of the side-effects of the success of *Holy Grail* was that sufficient money flowed in to allow him to take a year off from show-business and turn to a passion that had been with him since schooldays – Chaucer. The resulting book, *Chaucer's Knight*, offered fresh perceptions of the Knight in *The Canterbury Tales*, but invoked a certain amount of academic disdain. Jones had treated his subject in a historical, rather than a literary, sense, relating textual references to the fourteenth century itself, and was thus able to show that the knight, far from being the gallant, chivalrous figure normally depicted, was a hardened, callous mercenary. To write the book he invested in a collection of Chaucerian source material which included a number of rare texts, and a wall of his study is lined with bookshelves containing hundreds of volumes on the period. There is a smaller section devoted to another of his obsessive enthusiasms, Buster Keaton, whom he regards as the greatest comic genius of the cinema. He spends time lecturing schools and universities on both topics. A third interest of more recent activation is Rupert, the anthropomorphic bear in a woolly sweater and plaid trousers who has been in every issue of the *Daily Express* since 1920. Terry Jones remembers a boyhood interest in Rupert which was rekindled when

he bought some old annuals in a second-hand bookshop for his children to enjoy. He became excited by the work of Alfred Bestall who had been the artist of Rupert during the strip's heyday, having taken it over from its originator, Mary Tourtel, when her eyesight failed. Bestall proved to be alive and well, living in the Welsh mountains not so far from where Terry Jones was born, a spry and alert nonagenarian who turned out to be the star of a documentary film for Channel 4. *The Rupert Bear Story*, directed and narrated by Terry Jones, was transmitted for the first time in December 1982.

Another project which gave him a great deal of pleasure was the collection of fairy tales he wrote to amuse his daughter Sally, and which were published for Christmas 1981 in an edition lavishly illustrated by Michael Foreman. The fairy story is a minor literary form but nevertheless requires considerable discipline, for no matter how grotesque the elements within a tale are, the ironies and truths must be

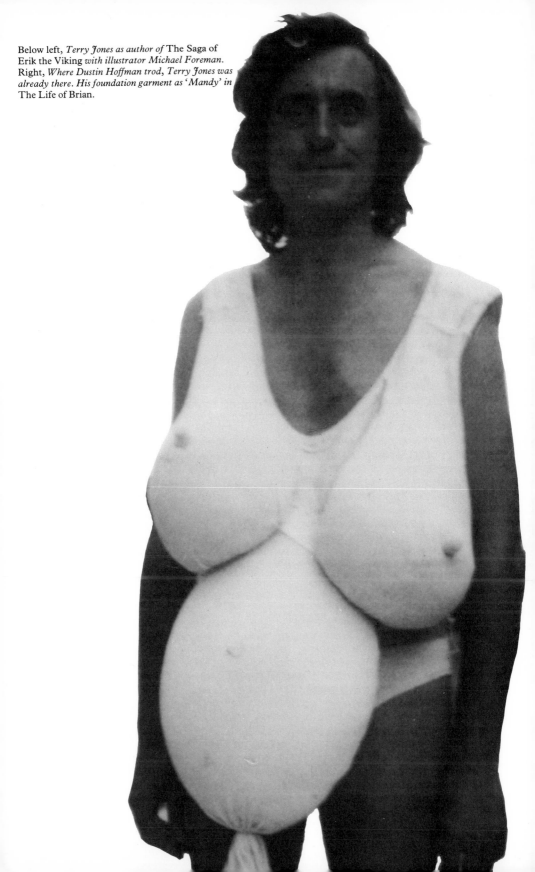

Below left, *Terry Jones as author of* The Saga of Erik the Viking *with illustrator Michael Foreman.* Right, *Where Dustin Hoffman trod, Terry Jones was already there. His foundation garment as 'Mandy' in* The Life of Brian.

immediately discernible for the child, so that he or she can find a point of identity in a make-believe world. Some of the stories were funny, others have a chilling dread, as effective as any of the excesses of the Brothers Grimm. And many ended with a satisfying twist. He has recently completed a further collection of children's stories entitled *The Saga of Erik the Viking*, and this time they were written for his son Bill.

Within the Python group Terry Jones is regarded as the counterpart of John Cleese. It is more than an Oxford–Cambridge split – John is a logician who believes that comedy works best if it is escalated through ordered phases. Much of the brilliance of John Cleese's television series, *Fawlty Towers* lay in the careful orchestration of separate incidents to achieve a disharmonious whole and a comic climax. Terry's style is much more unpredictable, and he is adept at bizarre juxtaposition. Each perfectly complements the other and the fourth television series suffered from John's absence in more ways than the mere lack of his presence. Terry, missing the scornful demolition of his ideas from John in script meetings, assumed the leadership, often bulldozing material through because the others were disinclined to engage in the daunting task of arguing. Terry's enthusiasm in full flight is an awesome monster to bring down. There are other contrasts, too. John has an aversion to the technical aspects of film-making and has no more idea of how a piece of celluloid passes through a camera than he has of nuclear physics. Terry, on the other hand, is fascinated by such mechanical essentials, and enjoys the laborious process of editing. John has a 'take it or leave it' attitude towards the Pythons and would lose no sleep were the team never to reassemble again. Terry, on the other hand, is like the Captain of a bored 1st XI keeping the team spirit alive as though his whole being depended on it, and expends ceaseless energy to do so. Yet each, in spite of years of conflict, has a deep-seated admiration for the other and is generous when talking about him.

As an indicator of their polarities it is interesting to note that John regarded the most recent film, *The Meaning of Life*, as an unmitigated nightmare during production, with discomforts and frustrations multiplying daily. Terry Jones, on the other hand, felt that it went like a dream, far more smoothly than any of the earlier works.

It was decided early in 1983 to advance the opening date in the United States, from a summer to a spring release, and much intensive work had to be put in during the preceding winter to meet the schedule. In February a preview was arranged in a shopping mall cinema in Yonkers, NY in order to measure public reaction, and to the consternation of some of the Universal executives, who had not interfered with the Pythons creatively during the making, the response was poor. Luckily, no great significance was attached to it, and the film opened properly at the end of March, having already received an excellent review in *Time*. Within the first eleven days of its release in 330 theatres across America it had taken what *Variety* would call a boffo $5½ million, setting it well on the road to profitability.

Notwithstanding his multitudinous array of talents – as a film director, a writer, a medieval historian, a comic performer and mime artist – Terry Jones is refreshingly normal. He is a worrier, and will expend as much sympathy and concern for the problems of those around him as he will for his own. His natural air of concern tends to make him a target for people with problems. He crams much into his days, running frantically through a crowded schedule. He is voluble, and when an idea is surfacing the arms wave and the words come too fast, degenerating into an incoherent series of falsetto squeals. He is warm, generous and fundamentally a kind man, who will defer, rather than give offence. He's the reliable pillar of strength and given the success of *The Meaning of Life*, it will be he who will get the ball rolling in a year or two's time, doggedly overcoming whatever reluctance he encounters.

Above, *Directing the sex lesson sequence in* The Meaning of Life *with John Cleese. Below, Terry Jones en famille in Camberwell with his wife, Alison and children Sally and Bill.*

TERRY GILLIAM

Terry Gilliam, sixth from left,
front row in his Fraternity House group,
Occidental College, Los Angeles, 1960.

A FEW YEARS AGO Terry Gilliam returned to the fine city of his birth, Minneapolis, in the heart of the American midwest. He screened his film *Jabberwocky* to a vast student audience at the University of Minnesota, in the largest auditorium on the campus. He had agreed to conduct a seminar on the making of the film and its relationship to Bosch, Brueghel and Samuel Beckett. Apprehensively, as the lights came up, he took his place on the podium and awaited the first question. In the audience a bespectacled arts major grasped the handheld microphone and said: "Mr Gilliam, sir. Would you mind telling us where you got your shoes?"

It was an appropriate query. A thesis could be written on Terry Gilliam and feet. His feet. Everyone's feet. The most vivid image in his animated opening credit sequence for the *Monty Python* shows was that of a large bare foot, lifted from a painting by the Tuscan artist Bronzino of Venus and Cupid, crashing down from the top of the screen. His own feet tend to be shod in shabby sneakers, although the footwear that so bemused the students at Minnesota U. were thick-soled Kickers in a particularly bilious shade of fluorescent yellow, a sight at that time unknown in the United States.

He spent his childhood in the rural surroundings of Medicine Lake, a hamlet on the western side of Minneapolis, which before the construction of Interstate 494 was deep in impenetrable country. "I've never got living in the country out of my blood, it's something you can't get away from. The secret hideaways, the swamp, the moss-lined caves, tree houses. We had a little house on a dirt road, woods behind the house – it was a real Tom Sawyer, Huckleberry Finn upbringing. One of my earliest memories is running through the woods with a friend barefoot, and we went into a shack where a nail went through his foot and impaled him – I had to run home and get my father to pull it out."

Life in the wintry wilds of Minnesota is not always directly comparable with that in London's Home Counties or Connecticut. The Gilliam's house had outside sanitation in the 1940s and answering a call of nature when the temperature was forty below called upon astonishing re-

serves of endurance. When an indoor toilet was finally installed he turned the outdoor one into a tree house some forty feet up, and he remembers another boyhood winter sport was to leap from it into a snowdrift far below making, fortunately, an unsuccessful grab at some high tension power lines on the way down.

Terry Gilliam was born on 22 November, 1940. His father was a travelling salesman for Folger's Coffee, a job that he quit in order to become a carpenter. He had originally come from Tennessee, but served in the last cavalry unit in the United States Army and ended up based in Minneapolis, where he decided to stay on returning to civilian life. Terry was the firstborn; he was followed by his sister two years later, and his younger brother in 1950, who is now a detective in the Los Angeles Police Department. In 1951 the family had migrated from Minnesota to California, eventually settling in the amorphous Los Angeles township of Panorama City. "I believed that I was going to see cowboys and Indians – it was a great disappointment. We went for several reasons – my sister was asthmatic and needed drier air. By then my father was with Johns-Manville, who were all over the States. The sad thing is that he was a very good carpenter, and he ended up making nothing else but office partitions."

Young Gilliam moved on to Birmingham High School where he modestly claims he found that as a consequence of abysmally-low educational standards he was able to attain straight As for most of the time, and still get his letter for pole-vaulting, be president of the student body, king of the senior prom, and the student most likely to succeed, without expending much visible effort. In those days he sported a crewcut of such severity that he looked like an inmate of a Marine Corps boot camp. From Birmingham High he moved on to Occidental College, where he worked his way through with a variety of jobs including one on the assembly line of the local Chevrolet plant. He decided that although the money was good it simply wasn't worth the energy expended. He had already developed considerable skill in drawing, and had learned how to take short cuts to achieve effective results. It

Above left, *Christmas in Panorama City, 1952. The young Terry discovers magic.* Left, *High School illustration by Terry Gilliam.* Above, *Working his way through college modelling campus clothing, 1960.* Right, *The Art Director takes a plunge. Gilliam on* Help! *cover, May, 1965.* Far right, *Clowning around with Terry Jones for the City Center show in New York.*

was a skill that would help to pay the rent on many subsequent occasions. He began life at Occidental as a Physics major, having a bent for science and mathematics, but after six weeks he switched to Fine Arts in the hope that it would be less boring, only to find that the professor in charge was able to make it even duller. Eventually he became a Political Science major, since the course was so fragmented and suited him, not only bestowing a liberal education, but allowing time for him to become interested in the college humour magazine.

"There was a group of us who became the campus clowns – it was before the word 'happening' came into use, but that's what we were doing, trying to shock and entertain everyone else on the campus." Among the pranks was to concoct an entirely bogus school history and repertoire of traditional rituals which were instilled into the freshmen to the confusion of future generations. He joined a fraternity (Sigma Alpha Epsilon) because it seemed a worthwhile thing to do, but almost immediately became disillusioned, and worked out a unique deal to take part only in the fun events in exchange for designing their graphic material.

The years at Occidental concluded with him graduating by the narrowest of margins, in view of the pressure of extra-curricular interests, which did not, it must be added, include the standard romantic entanglements. "I had incredibly high standards – I actually believed in love in those days. It had to be the right person, nothing less than the best, and it took time to find the best, time which I didn't have. I left college as pure as the driven snow – it was quite awful!"

In his last year he had been sending samples of his cartooning work in the college humour magazine to Harvey Kurtzman in New York, and his magazine *Help!* Having received what he took to be an encouraging response, he decided to emulate the young Moss Hart, whose autobiography, *Act One*, he had just been reading, and go off to New York in the hope of meeting his equivalent of George S. Kaufman. So he signalled his intention, and in spite of warnings by Kurtzman that work was hard to come by, he made the journey. Kurtzman was creating a comic strip for *Playboy* called *Little Annie Fanny* and had taken a suite at the Algonquin, the hotel on West 44th Street so closely associated with the interwar

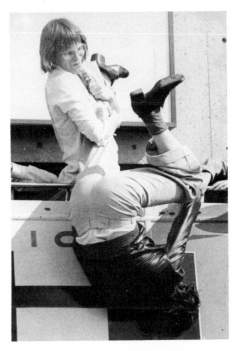

New York literati, which he had filled with several eminent cartoonists who were Terry Gilliam's idols. Furthermore, an editorial vacancy had just occurred on *Help!* with the resignation of Charles Alverson, and it was offered to the new kid in from the west. Gilliam spent three years working for the magazine, extending his range, and learning on a low salary to lay out and design material for it. It was during this period that he met John Cleese, in town for *Cambridge Circus*, and inveigled him into modelling for a photographic comic strip. There was, however, a looming shadow – the draft. By registering for the National Guard he had managed to escape its full horror, but was nevertheless called away for several months of basic training at Fort Dix, New Jersey. Through his talent for drawing he soon learned to evade arduous duties by creating flattering caricatures of the officers. He worked on the camp newspaper and learned the art of filling time and appearing to be active while doing as little as possible, a common army skill which he found difficult to shake off when it was all over. Finding that going back to *Help!* meant that he would be earning less money than if he had remained out-of-work and claimed social security benefits, he made the decision to leave New York, the United States, North America and took off for Europe and several months of hitchhiking. It was an eye-opening tour. He bought a secondhand motor cycle, the misbehaviour of which finally drove him to pushing it over the edge of a Spanish cliff in an act of execution. Having run out of money, he worked for a while on *Pilote* magazine in Paris for Réné Goscinny. "Being a cartoonist is the next best thing to being a musician. Just as it doesn't matter about language if you can strum a guitar, it's the same with cartooning if you get into a tight spot. When I was hitchhiking I had this huge hand made out of card, and I'd get a lift in no time at all. Even if people didn't pick me up they would laugh and wave, so I never felt totally alone out there."

Eventually he returned to New York and lived in Harvey Kurtzman's attic, trying to decide whether or not he should stay in America. He then returned to Los Angeles and worked as a freelance illustrator, later in an advertising agency. Becoming frustrated with the trivial output and the inefficiencies of clients, he remembered his army training and resolved to do as little work as possible, merely making a token appearance at the office each day, until he felt obliged to resign. The company, however, beat him to it by one day and fired him. He was by then living with Glenys Roberts, a British freelance journalist who was in Los Angeles recovering from a broken marriage, and at her urging he moved to London, attempting to tune in to the market for illustrators. Although his work was published in many places, including *The Sunday Times Magazine*, he found it a hard way to make a living. It was then that he worked for a short-lived magazine based on the formula of the successful publication, *New York*, called *The Londoner*, as art director, and saw it into an early demise.

"When that failed I was really low – it seemed impossible to get anywhere with magazines, so I called John Cleese and asked him how I could get into television. He suggested contacting Humphrey Barclay. Eventually I got to him. He was only mildly amused by my written sketches, but when I mentioned that I was a cartoonist he was interested. It helped, Humphrey being a cartoonist. Somehow he found room for one or two things I had written in *Do Not Adjust Your Set*, which did not endear me to Michael Palin or Terry Jones. Suddenly this interloper arrived on the scene with a couple of sketches they didn't like forced down their throats. Eric Idle was the nice one – he took me under his wing. Eric is very good with new people, and quick to befriend them. Then Humphrey went over to London Weekend when they started up. We did a wonderful show with Frank Muir and when we got through it we were told that no one saw it because there had been a dispute and the whole thing was blacked – it wasn't even videotaped. The idea was that I had to sit there each week doing

Assorted Gilliam graphics for Monty Python. *Note* Bronzino *foot, centre, borrowed from* Venus and Cupid, *top right.*

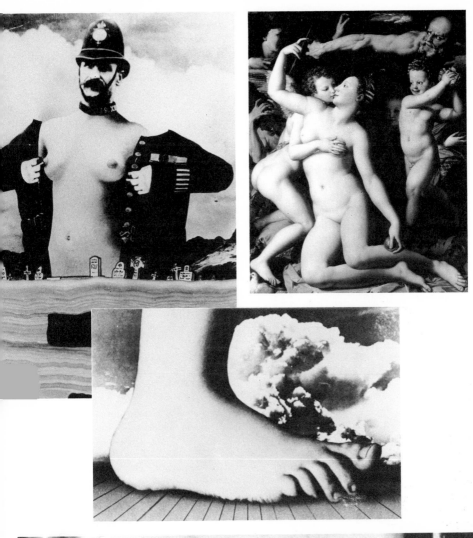

these cartoons, and there was this group – Eric, Benny Green, Katharine Whitehorn, Jenny Hanley, Frank Muir, Dick Vosburgh and myself, the gang. I had some Vaseline plastic shoes – they once got a closeup on the show – the shoes that Michael Palin wouldn't allow me to wear into their house. I had found them in France somewhere – I'd never known shoes to get such a definite reaction! All these desperate things to get attention – I've grown out of that now. But it was that moment of realising the power of television. You did something and suddenly ten million people had seen it and were commenting on it.

"I knew the techniques of animation in theory, having read a book or two, but I had never done anything in practice. The cutout technique I had seen years earlier in New York. It was fast and crude. If I had been given the money and time I would probably have tried to do a Walt Disney style. I think I was good with sound effects and the timing. The noises are fifty per cent of the effect.

"I still find it difficult to explain to the group that what I do needs all the elements before it works – like the 'Pirates' sequence in *The Meaning of Life*. When I tell them that when I put this noise on, or that sound effect, it's going to

We Have Ways of Making You Laugh, *1968 with Terry Gilliam, Benny Green, Margo Roche, Frank Muir, Dick Vosburgh, Eric Idle and Katherine Whitehorn.*

work, they don't really believe me because they can't imagine. It's only when it's done that they see it."

Because Terry Gilliam's contribution to *Monty Python* has been largely in supplying animated graphics (although he appeared as many memorable characters such as Cardinal Fang) his true genius lay in the astonishing link sequences in which rows of terrace houses would fly through the sky like geese, or giant feet would hold cities to ransom. He was spared the ritual ordeal of reading out his material in the weekly script sessions.

"I have never developed the presentation skills that the others have had to develop. They got better and better because before they could present their stuff to the audience they first had to present it to the group, which was very demanding. The only skill I had was to be able to do it, and ultimately let the result speak for itself. I didn't have to sell it. But even people like Terry Jones and Mike who were the most sympathetic – when I'd tell them over the phone what I was doing there would be these embarrassed silences. It would be necessary for me to produce the finished article before they'd know what I was talking about. But in a way I don't want to learn those skills – they can actually take away from the finished effort."

The other advantage he had was that because time was so short the work was often not completed until the very last minute, rendering dissection and criticism futile, since any hold-up would have prevented the programme from being taped on time, and he was by no means the first to discover the benefits of a tight deadline in getting work through untrammelled. "I'd literally work day and night when we were doing a series. The BBC had an excellent rostrum camera set-up. I'd be going seven days a week, usually with two all-nighters, churning out artwork, then go down there to play with it under the camera."

An avid buyer of art books, he would leaf through the pages looking for suitable images and then have them photographed. His collages were not made by cutting up original plates, contrary to the prevailing

Right, *Directing* Jabberwocky, *Shepperton, 1976.* Below, *some of the cast of the film with Max Wall as the King.*

opinion. "I have far too much respect for books to cut them up - I'd have pages photographed so that I could blow them up to any size and mess about with them. I like to think that when people go into the National Gallery and see the Bronzino that they'll look at the foot of Cupid and think 'Where have I seen that foot?' The fact that it's Cupid makes it all the funnier."

He believes that the choice of Sousa's jaunty march, *Liberty Bell*, as the Pythons' theme tune also arose through one of his creative sessions, although he thinks that it was Roger Last, the Python production assistant, who suggested it while they were playing through a number of records seeking the one that would best set the mood for the title animations. Memories are often hazy as to how such moments of history come to pass.

The Python's graphic style, applied not just to their television programmes, but to books, record albums, films, stage shows and assorted memorabilia owes much to the Gilliam imagination, and his ability to render in pictures the fantastic visualisations of other members of the group. When it was decided that the Pythons would control their own work, following their experience with their first film, *And Now for Something Completely Different*, it was also regarded as appropriate that Terry Gilliam and Terry Jones, both of whom were interested in the technical aspects of film-making and editing, would do the directing.

On *Monty Python and the Holy Grail* the duo achieved a reasonable result in the face of logistical and budgetary problems, but Terry G. found the experience less satisfactory than Terry J., and so on the next film, *The Life of Brian*, he let the latter get on with it. But meanwhile he had made *Jabberwocky* from a screenplay he had written with his old friend Charles Alverson, with Michael Palin playing the lead in a medieval setting. Gilliam was anxious that it should not be thought of as a Python film, although the American distributors openly stated a link. The film was only moderately successful, and audiences found the predilection for the gor-

John Cleese as Robin Hood and the six dwarfish Time Bandits.

ier, dirtier aspects of life in those times disturbing. Gilliam looks askance at the Hollywood convention that everyone in a costume film should seem bandbox fresh, and had perhaps gone too far in the opposite direction, allowing Palin to appear as a Candide picking his way through mountains of frightful ordure.

The disappointment of *Jabberwocky* was assuaged by the much more cheerful reception of *Time Bandits*, although there were several dissenting London critics. Gilliam had really wanted to make an adventure that would appeal to children. Hence the central character, a small boy, Kevin, taken by a gang of marauding, picaresque dwarfs on a series of time trips where they meet such characters as Napoleon, played by Ian Holm, Robin Hood (John Cleese) and Agamemnon (Sean Connery). The culminating duel between Good, as personified by Sir Ralph Richardson, and Evil, David Warner, further exemplifies the simplistic fairytale morality. There is an odd relationship between the dwarfs and the boy because they are all the same height. The attraction of the story to children is strong, a juvenile mind being much more capable of assimilating the sudden switches of locale and plot as the adventurers hurtle on their hare-brained flips through the temporal dimension. In the United States the film was a major success, bringing in valuable revenue for HandMade Films - the company formed by George Harrison and Denis O'Brien which had backed the project - and undoubtedly served to attract studio finance for the next Python Python movie.

When *The Meaning of Life* reached production it had been decided that Terry Gilliam would have a hand in the direction, not alongside Terry Jones, but in charge of a special section, known as "the other unit". Given the most handsome of budgets he had ever commanded, Gilliam devised an ambitious sequence, part of which involved model animation, wherein a staid, traditional insurance company, peopled by elderly employees working with antiquated office equipment, suddenly turned on their new young masters who had taken them over as part of their multi-national conglomerate. Using filing cabinets as cannon, fan blades as cutlasses, hat racks as grappling hooks, the aged clerks vanquish their oppressors, and then turn to financial piracy, setting out to storm the commercial bastions of the world. To the strains of bogus Korngold they lift anchor and set sail through the curtain-walled canyons of glass and steel in their old-fashioned Edwardian baroque office building. A marvellous, crazy idea, it has the grandiose and nonsensical absurdity that probably only Terry Gilliam would have the audacity to translate to the screen. Initially, his sequence was to form a section in the middle of the film, but early previews showed that it overbalanced and stopped the flow, making an unnecessary caesura. There was some anxiety as to how things could be resolved. The solution was to detach it completely from the main film, and make it into a separate short which would precede it wherever *The Meaning of Life* was shown. A small reference to it was also retained in the film proper, as an attempt by the second feature to hijack its superior.

After *The Meaning of Life*, which for him was a protracted and demanding experience (he had been apprehensive at returning to animation for the main and end title sequences feeling that it was a retrogressive move), Gilliam embarked on a new project, called *Brazil* after the song, rather than the place, with the screenplay written by Tom Stoppard. "It's really about Walter Mitty meeting Franz Kafka," said Gilliam in an attempt to encapsulate the paranoid plot which had become too labyrinthine for coherent description. He found the experience of working with Stoppard curiously unnerving in that the playwright insisted on going off to write by himself rather than attempt to hammer out ideas jointly. "He's not used to working in collaboration, and I'm not used to working not in collaboration," says Gilliam. "Mike Palin will play the villain, for once. When he does the dirty it will be so much more frightening."

As far as future projects are concerned Gilliam is sure that they will occur. "I cannot visualise a time when we wouldn't do something together," he said. "We're tied in so many ways, not just in busi-

ness." He places himself alongside the Oxford section of the team, with Terry Jones and Michael Palin. "We're the workhorses, the sloggers, the guys who really sweat it out to get it right. We're the ones who stay up all night in the cutting room. John and Graham and Eric come in and do what they have to do brilliantly, then walk away from it. It's true that the Oxford men are the romantics, the Cambridge ones the pragmatists. They're really ruthless. They know just what they want." His alignment with Oxford could be said to follow from his own university being *Occi*dental, with the same initial syllable as smart alecs have occasionally pointed out. In fact, the western temperament finds an easier association with the Oxonian attitude. But like all the Pythons, and being the only non-Oxbridge member of the team he is probably in the best position to appreciate it, he regards the polarities and differences as essential to their success, producing an abrasive interaction which results in distinctive, unsettling and surrealistic comedy.

How does someone with Terry Gilliam's monomaniacal drive find time to get married, have children and retain the semblance of a private life? Iain Johnstone, who has made a number of television documentaries about the team and has known them for several years, believes that Python is a destroyer of marriages unless the women are prepared to take second place. The plight of the Python wife is comparable with that of the captain's wife played by Celia Johnson in Noël Coward's celebrated British war film *In Which We Serve*, when in a moving Christmas speech she acknowledges that her husband is also married to his ship, and that she will always have to yield to her rival.

Terry Gilliam's wife, Maggie, was the make-up girl on the Python shows. "The romance blossomed on location in Torquay - a magic place! For years people didn't know we were married. Even my parents didn't know we were married. Maggie is a bit more traditional than me, and getting married meant more to her. I don't even actually know the date it happened - I think the month was October and the place Belsize Park. I hate those things other people place such importance on, it becomes their property somehow, rather than the two people who are actually involved."

The Gilliams live in a tall Victorian house on the south edge of Hampstead Heath, the front door reached by a steep, curving flight of steps. The interior has been remodelled to create space and light, and the Gilliam studio is at the top, a custom-built loft area with big windows and a spectacular view. The house is dotted with artefacts that have been used in various films – a giant cotton-reel, for example, bigger than a child, or the intricate model of the Crimson Permanent Assurance Building from *The Meaning of Life*. They have two daughters, Amy aged six and Holly, two. Maggie still works on the make-up for the Python films, which is sufficient to keep her career ticking over, and her husband is anxious that she should not, as so many successful career women are forced to, become merely a housewife and mother.

Having lived in Britain since the sixties he has no great desire to return permanently to the country of his birth, although he makes frequent visits there in the course of his business and to see his widowed mother in Los Angeles. Terry Gilliam can be regarded as an expatriate American who has made a sizeable and significant contribution to British culture, and who has allowed himself to be assimilated by what he regards as a more casual lifestyle which allows him to get on with whatever he wants to do without the pressures of keeping up a public face. Intensely creative, nervously twitchy, he speaks rapidly and fluently, ideas constantly tumbling forth and disappearing into absurdity just as quickly. Charles Alverson who has known Terry longer than anyone else in Britain says that no one really knows him, that he conceals much more than he ever reveals. "Perhaps Terry doesn't even really know himself." Their relationship is much cooler after a screenplay collaboration that went wrong. He believes that the Gilliam ambition may eventually mess him up, especially if it drives him back to America to make his films.

Terry Gilliam admits that he suffers from creative frustration a lot of the time. He will work hard and long to find that something is to no avail, then stare moodily out of the window. A day without a significant result will exacerbate his gloom. At such times he is not an easy man. But when he is on form, and knows it, there is a touch of genius about his output. He needs pressure to succeed, and distrusts the mellowing effects of middle age. Like the other Pythons he is extremely critical of the things that they have done outside the group – in particular the film *Privates on Parade*, with John Cleese, which he considers was poorly photographed and constructed. It is one of the nicest things about the Pythons in general that they are not necessarily polite about one another, but are forceful in saying what they believe. It is also what makes their working together a stimulating, infuriating, challenging nightmare to be entered into sparingly. Hence their separate ways. "But there's something between us that's very important," says Gilliam. "We'll be back!"

Terry Gilliam on location directing Time Bandits.

85

JOHN CLEESE

IT IS ONE OF those boring axioms that great clowns are fundamentally serious men. John Cleese is a subscriber to the theory and, unlike everyone else, doesn't regard himself as particularly funny. He readily admits to a troubled hyperactive temperament coupled with stress and depression in his life at various stages, but he also contends that after years of psychotherapy he is sunnier, mellower, more contented and master of his inner self. He spent three and a half years in group sessions with Robin Skynner, and so impressed with their effect was he that he determined to co-author a book in order that others could find relevance and interest in some of the ideas. "A lot of them were very new – and there didn't seem to be any other place where you could find them, except in a very feeble and diluted form in *Cosmopolitan*. There didn't seem to be anywhere where you were treated intelligently, but non technically. I suggested to Robin that we should make some television programmes, but then we found that no one in television is interested in ideas – they're only interested in whether it's going to make nice pictures or not. So we decided to go for book form.

"It happens to be what I'm primarily interested in. Johnson – 'the proper study of man is man' – that sort of thing. I've always found it a bit hard to see how anyone could get obsessed with electronics, geology and motorbikes, yet any facet of how people behave seems to me to be fascinating, so I go for history, psychology, psychiatry and a bit of religion as well. The other thing is that if you start seeing better how you work, you start seeing better how everyone else works, so the respectable excuse is to say that it's terribly helpful to my writing, but that's not actually why I do it. I do it because I'm interested."

Cleese lives in a handsome Victorian house in Ladbroke Road, not far from the Holland Park tube station. He has tamed it room by room every time his accountant has given the green light for more work to be done. He lives there with his second wife Barbara and sometimes his daughter Cynthia whom he shares with Connie, his first wife, now living in Hampstead.

Around the corner he maintains a separate office. It is really a shop, and because of zoning laws must remain looking like one. The main floor is ruled by his attractive secretary, Daphne Day, who besides coping with the prolific output of words from her boss, has occasionally to pretend that the place is a gallery, although only one of the items on view, which include a number of Python artefacts, is for sale. It is a Cezanne print, outrageously overpriced at £290 plus V.A.T. Down a narrow staircase, in a low-ceilinged windowless basement room, John Cleese works behind a table which almost fills the available space. Most of the Pythons favour spacious, sunlit studies at the tops of their houses; only Cleese works in a bare, subterranean room with no outlook.

He is so tall that when he stands his head brushes the ceiling. He is lean, rugged, fit, still possessing, in spite of a thick black beard, looks that George Melly once described as "inanely handsome".

Meeting him there as distinct from meeting him socially reinforces the impression noted by others that he is very like an established lawyer, and might very well have turned out to have been one. "At school I had Science A-levels – Mathematics, Physics and Chemistry – which is rather bizarre. I had two years teaching when I did English, History and Geography, at the end of which I realised I was never going to compete with the scientists at Cambridge, who were highly motivated. Science for me was something I had been put into because I was a reasonable mathematician. So I looked around for what I could escape into. It was terribly funny – there was a family tradition of law, which I took quite seriously. I didn't really examine it until I found out that it meant that my grandfather had been a solicitor's clerk! I never had any ambition to be a barrister, that was a bit upmarket for me. I think that I could have done it pretty well, actually. My strength is in argument, because I've got a good line in logic, and a very good line in dismounting bad arguments. I think I'm most amusing when I'm ridiculing other people's arguments – I don't think of myself as amusing ordinarily, but if I'm in an argument with someone I'm quite good at touching the weak points. But barristers work so hard. They're the most compulsive workers of the lot – they flog themselves. They're strange creatures because they get so transported into the realm of words that they tend more than any other profession I've come across to lose contact with their feelings. It was very revealing that barristers turned up most in group therapy – more lawyers than anyone else."

Cleese was born on 27 October, 1939 at Weston-super-Mare, then in the county of Somerset, but now part of Avon, which embraces the nearby city of Bristol. Weston is a quiet Victorian resort on the Bristol Channel, its houses for the most part constructed of the grey Mendip limestone from the nearby hills. It lies between

two headlands, and is renowned for the virtual disappearance of the sea twice a day when the tide goes out, leaving an expanse of jelly-like dun-coloured mud. His parents were both middle-aged, in their forties. His father, an insurance salesman, had sensibly changed his family name from Cheese when he joined the army in the First World War. Both parents made considerable sacrifices to pay for their son's private education, initially at St Peter's Preparatory School in Weston, then at Clifton College where he was a day boy. He found that there was an unspoken social prejudice practised by the boarders, who felt that the day boys were not one hundred per cent part of the scene.

"I was something of an outsider. I was immensely tall – I was six feet tall when I was twelve, and by the time I got to Clifton I remember being measured for my Corps uniforms, I suppose in my second term, and I was $6'4\frac{3}{4}''$ then. I remember being astounded that I was so tall. I haven't grown upwards since, I've just put on about six stone. I was your original seven stone weakling. At that height I was physically awkward because I was weak. You can't move well, or play games well if you don't have the strength – I realised that even as late as Cambridge. Much as I loved soccer I could never really play it because I just could not turn fast enough.

"The problem of being tall was that it was always hard to fade into the background. I remember a master making a joke about me being a prominent citizen and thought it was a compliment, and then getting a laugh out of the form by saying that he meant that I stuck out a lot. I always had this outsider status, which I think has gone on for years. It's a bit like my relationship with show-business – I don't feel that I'm one hundred per cent in it. I was an immensely meek boy, and I was bullied a lot. I remember my father coming down to watch me play in a football match and finding three people sitting on me. I had a lot of problems about asserting normal healthy aggression. I think that went on for a long time; even at Clifton when I was playing soccer I didn't like the violent side of it, and if someone kicked me, almost on a point of principle I wouldn't kick them back. It's taken me

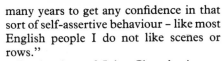

John Cleese during his days at Cambridge.

many years to get any confidence in that sort of self-assertive behaviour – like most English people I do not like scenes or rows."

In the days of John Cleese's time at Clifton the fees were a mere £60 a term, and later by winning a Mathematics scholarship worth £36 per annum he reduced his father's outlay to £48 a term. As a consequence of his academic prowess he was put in a scholarship form, where he distinguished himself in English and Latin. "I always performed well in exams – I think because I was reasonably organised and a bit cynical about them, I saw what they were about. I didn't have any illusions, so I went for them in a cold-blooded way and got good results.

"Nobody in my family had ever been near a university, but my father, who was an immensely kind man, let me stick to my intention, and somehow found the money for a final year at school during which I sat the entrance exam for Downing College at Cambridge. I had to wait two years before I could go, as they had just abolished National Service and were deluged with people. Because I had been brought up in cotton wool, instead of getting out of the country to go away and learn a language, I was so unenterprising

I retired away to Weston-super-Mare to teach at my old prep school, and I went up to Cambridge at twenty-one."

By then he had decided to switch to reading Law, having observed the dedication of Cambridge scientists. He also made an attempt to get into the Footlights. "When I was about eleven I had discovered that I could make the other kids laugh. And at Clifton, in a quiet and rather cowardly way, because I never had the balls to be really naughty, I could still make people laugh with subversive comments. Towards the end of my time there I did one or two house entertainments and house plays which had comedy in them, and in my last term I wrote a Stanley Unwin-type nonsense piece, and a wonderfully insulting piece on my housemaster. I was always very intrigued and interested in comedy shows. I was a tremendous fan of American shows in the fifties like Burns and Allen, Bilko, Amos n' Andy – although I didn't care for *I Married Joan* and *I Love Lucy*. Then I discovered the Marx Brothers, and I got intrigued by Hancock – and *The Goon Show*, of course. I was obsessive about *The Goon Show*. Two or three of the sketches in my last term at Clifton were rather spectacular – we did a Nazi thing, because I was always able to do cod-German and I played Hitler, and we dragged someone out of the audience – he was a plant – and he disappeared through the door at the bottom of the school tower which slammed. And I went on with the German ranting and said how people would be punished if they behaved like that man, and suddenly there was a shout and right up at the top of the tower they threw a dummy, and people thought that we had really thrown this guy off. It was very well done. One or two people had said I ought to go into the Footlights, so when I got up to Cambridge I went along to the Societies' Fair they have at the Guildhall at the beginning of each academic year, and found the Footlights stand. They asked me if I sang. I was so bad at singing I wasn't allowed to do it at school. They then asked me if I could dance. Well, I had never danced in my life. They looked puzzled and said, 'What do you do?' I stammered and said that I tried to make people laugh, and it sounded so pathetically lame I blushed and rushed away and didn't go near them again for two terms.

"Then my closest friend, a guy called Alan Hutchison who is now a publisher, bumped into the Treasurer, who asked him to do something, so he mentioned me, and was told that we should try to write together. We sat down and produced three pieces, one of which was pinched from the funny columnist, Peter Simple, in the *Daily Telegraph* – a send-up of Montgomery, and one of which was pinched from a radio show, and one of which was a send-up of a news item. We went along and auditioned them and people seemed very friendly, then we did them in front of an audience and we were elected. But then I wrote some other pieces and they were so terrible I wasn't allowed to perform them. Their revue that year was called *I Thought I Saw It Move* which David Frost was in and I auditioned for it, but there wasn't any hope. But the funny thing was that when we came back the next term we wandered into the Footlights clubroom after about the second day, and found that we were on the committee because everyone else had left. Suddenly we were the big boys. What was so wonderful about the Footlights was that it was there and it had to be done. Whereas in Oxford they had to start from scratch and organise everything. Of course, all the people who are good at doing jokes and sketches are terrible at hiring lights. Humphrey Barclay was the only guy I've ever known who was good at both.

"I've always felt, speaking for my generation, that Cambridge people were more efficient. Oxford people tended to be woollier. Even to the way they dress. Michael Palin always wears softer kinds of clothes. They are often much less clear in their objectives. At Cambridge most groups, the politicians, the journalists, the straight actors, were very aware of London, and knew where they were going. Mind you, I don't think it was true of the Footlights in my year – I don't think there was a single one of them who seriously

John Cleese in Cambridge Circus, *cartoon by Humphrey Barclay.*

JOHN

AS THE PROSECUTING COUNSEL

92

contemplated going into show-business.

"I nearly didn't do *A Clump of Plinths*, the Footlights show that became *Cambridge Circus*. I fell in love, an extraordinary new experience, and I couldn't cope with it at all. I couldn't get any work done, and halfway through my second term I decided more or less not to do the revue because it didn't seem to matter. After all, I'd done it the year before when Trevor Nunn was directing. Then I remember thinking one weekend that I rather liked the blokes and that it would only be two weeks in Cambridge and we'd be finished, so I did it. I realised it was pretty good but didn't think it was all that special, and after about four days I went into the clubroom where we used to go after the show, and there were these two guys in grey suits, Peter Titheradge and Ted Taylor, and I suddenly realised they were asking if I wanted a job at the BBC. Then I discovered they'd offered one to Humphrey and to Bill (Oddie) - they were going for people who could be producers or writers. I was supposed to be joining a firm of solicitors in the City called Freshfields, at £12 a week, and here they were offering £30. I thought, why not? So I went with them. And then *Cambridge Circus* was signed for the West End. Suddenly we were young people who were successful and were having newspaper articles written about us!"

When the opportunity to tour New Zealand with *Cambridge Circus* arose it proved irresistible, and leave was sought from the BBC after about nine months working in radio comedy on script polishing. Apart from the novelty of the show having a resurrection after its West End run, the thought of an antipodean jaunt held a note of high adventure, somewhat dampened when reality loomed. "New Zealand was a hopelessly inefficient place. It's all to do with standards. If you don't know what's good you can't provide it. I remember Johnny Lynn and I going to the opening of a new restaurant in Christchurch. It was freezing. Johnny ordered a bottle of red wine, and it was brought to our table stone cold. Johnny said that at least it was at room temperature!"

After six weeks in New Zealand the team went on to Broadway, pausing for

about three days in England en route. "I was far more interested in being in New York than doing the show. We were falsely confident about it, and none of us appreciated the cultural gap. As we rehearsed we realised that the people who had invited us didn't know the first thing about our work, and there was a crisis. We were killed by the total lack of publicity and the fact that the *New York Times* sent a sports writer to review it. By the time Walter Kerr did his fantastic piece we had closed."

It was during this period that Terry Gilliam, then working for Harvey Kurtzman's humour magazine *Help!*, approached Cleese and got him to pose for his photographed comic strip in which a middle-class suburban man falls in love with a Barbie doll. "I liked him enormously," remembers Cleese, "and I think that he thought that I was good at mugging, which is supposed to be a sort of compliment."

After the show had transferred briefly to the Village, Cleese decided to stay on for a while in the United States. Asked to audition for a role in the Broadway musical *Half a Sixpence*, starring Tommy Steele, to his amazement he got the part, notwithstanding his total inability to sing. He was paid what to him seemed an astonishing $200 a week, and enjoyed the experience, although the director who had hired him was replaced by Gene Saks with whom he did not get on with very well. He mimed the chorus singing and the audience was none the wiser. Cleese's next venture was even stranger. He was talking to a man on a subway station who worked for *Newsweek* and expressed to him envy of a journalist's life. An introduction was immediately arranged to the International Editor, who offered Cleese a job. Then his sponsor was sent off on a long foreign assignment, and Cleese found himself trying to muddle along in an unfamiliar office with no basic journalistic training. He realised when he was given obituaries of living people to write that he was doomed, so he quit before being fired. Three days later he was offered the chance to appear in the touring show of *The Establishment*, which was then in Chicago. It occupied him until the end of 1965,

when he returned to England at the invitation of David Frost, who wanted him for *The Frost Report*.

Meanwhile, he had met Connie Booth in New York, where she was waiting tables between acting, jobs, as is so often the case with the thousands of young hopefuls who flock in from the Middle West as she had done. The courtship was lengthy, and she was unwilling to uproot herself for a new country when Cleese went back to England. They were obliged to conduct a transatlantic affair, seeing each other about twice a year, until the beginning of 1968 when they decided to get married. By this time Cleese was well-established in British television, and eventually they bought a house in Woodsford Square, a modern townhouse development amid the palatial Victorian villas of Holland Park. In 1971 their daughter Cynthia was born.

"Connie had the usual difficulties getting work, which were exacerbated by the fact that she had an American accent, but

Part of the photostrip devised by Terry Gilliam for Help! *in which Cleese played a suburbanite who fell for a Barbie doll.*

94

95

she sat down and worked very hard on that. By then I was doing Python and it was taking up ten months of the year. I had enjoyed the first series enormously, but the others wanted to hang on together, and I felt that it was like being married to Python. I was feeling very constricted and I wanted to get away. They all felt I was being disloyal when I quit, but I thought that was rather juvenile. I only wanted to do occasional television programmes, I didn't want to marry them!"

As the feeling of constriction increased Cleese left, leaving the Pythons to do the fourth series without him. Meanwhile, he started to work with Connie on fashioning a situation comedy series. *Fawlty Towers* is among the funniest shows ever developed for television, and embodies certain virtues which mark it as a classic – a simple basic idea, the setting in a small, resort hotel; rounded characterisation in that its central figure, the dreadful Basil, has shading that makes him an interesting personality, rather than a flat stereotype; well-drawn supporting characters, particularly Sybil Fawlty, the infuriatingly patient, capable wife played by Prunella Scales, with an unfailing ability to make any given situation worse. Although a lot of the comedy in *Fawlty Towers* was inspired farcical slapstick it also had sub-

tlety. It is the comedy of a drowning man clutching at straws, as the egregious, manic Basil seizes yet another insane notion to extricate himself from some ghastly predicament. There is a great deal of Basil Fawlty in many people, and Cleese admits that there have been times when he has bottled his irritation exactly like him, rather than screaming with rage and vexation. While the comic construc-

tion of the show was his, the delineation of the characters, particularly the women, owed much to Connie, who believed that Basil was funniest when he was most unpredictable. *Fawlty Towers* consisted of only two series of six episodes apiece; deliberately the decision was taken not to extend it further and risk it going flat.

Ironically, while the Cleese–Booth writing team was doing so brilliantly,

Left, *John Cleese and Connie Booth at work writing* Fawlty Towers. *Above and right, scenes from the two series. Cleese as Basil Fawlty; Andrew Sachs as Spanish waiter Manuel; Prunella Scales as Sybil Fawlty and Connie Booth as Polly.*

their marriage was not. "Connie and I started to get a bit rocky in about '74. We split once, got back together, split again and got back together, then split. The actual decision to end it completely was taken in New York when we were doing the Python stage show in '76. Having done the psychotherapy we don't think in terms of whose fault it was. It was very much a fifty-fifty thing. We stayed very good friends. About three years ago she moved to Hampstead. We share Cynth half-and-half. She's a markedly healthy, vigorous little girl. She often says that now I've married Barbara it's a bit like having two mothers.

"I met Barbara at a lunch when I was performing *Monty Python at the Hollywood Bowl*. It all happened very fast. We realised that there was something serious going on and I came back to London, and then we decided to get married. We actually got hitched in Los Angeles at her house in one of those funny American weddings where you hire a judge. It's rather nice, actually. I'd always assumed I would get married again because I think that it is the ideal state. I like it. I went through quite a lot of depression after my first marriage broke up, and it was fortunate that I was able to see Robin Skynner, and his therapy group. I learned how to handle depression – I'd always become hyperactive before, like Basil.

"It wasn't part of a pre-arranged plot that I should marry another American – it was just the way it happened. Someone had suggested that by marrying Americans I've solved the problem of not knowing where I was in the class system. I think it's much more that there's a very positive quality I like enormously about American women. When I met Barbara she had done so many different things – she had been an art major and was a talented painter. She had then married an Englishman, so we were both on our second tries. She worked at Sotheby's. Then she did the model-actress thing. And because she's very good at thinking on her feet she auditioned and against enormous competition got the job of front-of-camera reporter for CBS News. So she used to go off with a crew, direct, edit, write the commentary, deliver it – but she found that was a killer, being

a news junkie. She left that and directed films for television. I found this enormously attractive – that she could go out and boss twenty men around. She's even directed a couple of time for Video Arts. And now she's gone back to painting, which has always been her first love. I've often felt that about American women, that they are a little bit freer, a little more alive to the possibilities of what they could be doing, and I find that attractive.

"I'm beginning to see for the first time in my life what really interests me. Partly because I've worked bloody hard for twenty years with a lot of stress – I've never been out of work – and I've reached a point where I can take time off without financial worries. I can now do what I want to do. But then the problem arises to decide what that is.

"I find Python rather narrow. It was enormously exciting – we felt security in numbers, you never felt quite so exposed as you might do in a solo project, and there was a lot of good humour and camaraderie. But it's an envious group, of that there is no doubt, and there were a lot of resentments. Graham has come out and talked about the alcoholism now, but it is true to say that it was extremely difficult spending six hours a day with someone who was basically alcoholic. But I went through all that nasty period and then we had a very good time together on *The Life of Brian*, the most satisfactory project we have ever done. It was not the case on *The Meaning of Life*, where we would have no real starting point. I felt that it was a deeply frustrating experience and I didn't really enjoy it. I felt once or twice we had to go for a sketch film, and funnily enough, I couldn't get people to agree to that. We kept going round and round in circles and when we finally got out to the West Indies to settle it one way or the other, after a few days two or three of us were saying 'Let's forget it!' Five months had been spent getting nowhere, and during that time working singly or with one other Python I could have produced a whole movie. Then Terry Jones came down to breakfast one morning and really managed to energise it. By lunchtime we had the idea, and Graham and I clinched it by going off and writing a birth scene.

But the performing was not very enjoyable this time – Terry did a marvellous job making it look good, but half the time I felt I was just there to make a special effect look right."

John has a legendary reputation for being the grumbler of the group. Just as Terry Jones represents one polarity in the field of stoic endurance for the cause of film-making, so Cleese stands at the other, and once said that film acting was about as interesting as waiting for a flight at Heathrow for six weeks. He gained far more excitement in the five weeks spent rehearsing for the role of Petruchio in Jonathan Miller's BBC version of *The Taming of the Shrew* because it gave him an opportunity to explore his range as an actor. For similar reasons he relished his part in Michael Blakemore's film adaptation of *Privates on Parade* in which he played a knuckle-headed British major, the first role he had sustained in a film from beginning to end. He was incensed, however, that the television trailer for it leaned heavily on the silly walks he had performed after the end titles, thus giving a misleading impression of his performance. Cleese is a great admirer of Peter Nichols, who wrote the original play and the screenplay, and of a handful of other

John Cleese with his mother when she received an award for her radio commercial for Life of Brian.

British comic playwrights who include Michael Frayn, Alan Ayckbourn and Tom Stoppard.

But what of his future involvement with Python? "I would like to work individually with any one of them. But I cannot imagine any circumstances in which I would like to get back into that committee type of writing. When you get to forty-three you realise that time is beginning to run out and you can't do everything you want to do, so you have to focus a bit more. I found the committee work had no enjoyment for me on this last film. I love the company, I'd love to have lunch or dinner with them. But I'm not going to get to writing as well as David Hare, or Frayn, or Stoppard in committee.

"One of the things I have realised by observing my own behaviour a lot in the last few years is that I am not actually capable of predicting how I shall feel in a few months. I can make quite a lot more outside Python than I can in, and provided that I can always have meals with them I can't see any reason to work professionally. It's a function of age, isn't it? As you get older you want to run your own show a bit more!"

GRAHAM CHAPMA[N]

*Graham Chapman in school drama production
at Melton Mowbray Grammar School.*

ON THE FACE of it Graham Chapman appears to be the calmest of the Pythons, an effect he carefully cultivates by smoking a pipe, a well-known way to give the impression of a thoughtful listener. The circumstances of his birth were decidedly uncalm; he arrived on 8 January, 1941 in the middle of an air raid on the Midlands city of Leicester. He claims that he was not traumatised by it, but recalls an unpleasant wartime memory from the age of three. "My father was a policeman, at that stage a constable on the beat in a suburb of Leicester. He had to attend an air crash. There were a lot of pieces of aircraft and people. My father was sent along there to sort it out. I was taken there by my mother who was merely saying hallo to him while he was doing his job. A woman came out of the house carrying a bucket of what looked like liver, and probably was. And there were a number of ominous-looking sacks. That sort of thing would put you off war."

Graham Chapman's father stayed in the police force and eventually retired with the rank of chief-inspector. "He wasn't all that authoritarian. He believed in the spirit of the law, rather than the letter. He certainly wasn't the kind who chalks up lots of arrests to get promotion. He was pretty easy-going, really. I have to say that there are very few other policemen I've met I'd liked to have had as a father, though. His job didn't impinge on my life too much."

His brother, who was four years older, had decided to become a doctor, and the ambition transferred to the young Graham, who studied the books that were lying around the house. It ran in tandem with another aspiration. "From the age of about eight or nine I had been an avid listener to the radio, to all things comedic, and later I became a television watcher – Jewel and Warris, *Educating Archie*, the lot. Then around about the age of fourteen I saw an excerpt on TV of a Footlights Show, I think that Jonathan Miller may have been in it. So that slipped into my subconscious, and I thought that if I'm to do medicine then Cambridge is the university to go to."

As a policeman Chapman *père* was required to move around his county with successive postings, and so his younger son went to a number of different schools. The most important was Melton Mowbray Grammar School, in the pleasant market town famous for its succulent meat pies and its pet food factory. "I was comfortable at Melton Mowbray because it was a small town with its own identity, not a faceless Leicester suburb. At school I could do a lot of acting. There was a Gilbert and Sullivan every year, and a Shakespeare every year, and we also did revues. There were a lot of chances to go over the top. Then a new headmaster, a rather splendid guy called Brewster, encouraged me to go to Cambridge. One of the perks of being in the sixth form was to be able to do the show each year, which I tried to make slightly different, so that it wasn't just a series of impersonations of school masters."

Getting into Cambridge proved unexpectedly easy. He went for an interview at Emmanuel College, where the Master himself made a practice of seeing all the likely candidates. After a half-hour he was told he had a place, subject to good A-level marks, from the following October. His playing of rugby was approved, as were painting and drawing, but the head of the college warned him off acting, saying that there wouldn't be any time for that. "I'd been briefed that the way to pass the interview was to agree with him most of the time, but to disagree at one point, just to show I had a mind of my own. So that's where I differed."

He went up to Cambridge for the Michaelmas Term 1959, and within days of arrival hurried to the Societies' Fair that was staged to recruit freshmen into the side range of extracurricular activities. The Footlights had a stall, which was manned by David Frost, then club secretary. "I asked if I could join. He said 'No!' So I asked what the point was of having a stall and he said that there was none at all, really, and explained that if one wanted to join one had to be invited to audition. Being invited to audition seemed rather unattainable, so I joined the Mummers instead. Then I found another guy, called Anthony Branch, at the same college who was reading Law, and who was a bit of a pianist. We teamed up and hit on the idea

of holding our own smoking concert to which we invited the Footlights' committee, and we also provided a lot of good claret. They came to our smoker, which was quite a reasonable show, drank our claret, and thus we got our invitation to audition and were duly elected. But by then it was my second year. It was when I met John Cleese – he was auditioning at the same time. Afterwards we compared notes, went off to the Kenya Coffee House, and that's how the two of us came to work together. We wrote two or three sketches for smokers that year."

John Cleese arrived in Cambridge a year later than Graham Chapman, and achieved membership of the exclusive society in his first year. Eric Idle came up in the following year, and like Graham got into the Footlights following a satisfactory college smoker. As Robert Hewison has shown in his history of the club, it was at this stage riding on a peak of popular esteem, and by virtue of having its own clubroom and bar was an important social focus for Cambridge actors. In 1961–2 both Cleese and Chapman were on the committee, as registrar and member-without-portfolio respectively. *Double Take* in 1962 was the only May Week revue in which Graham Chapman appeared, under the direction of Trevor Nunn. On the stage with him were Tim Brooke-Taylor, Humphrey Barclay, Tony Hendra, Alan George, Miriam Margolyes, Nigel Brown, Robert Atkins and John Cleese. Humphrey Barclay remembers the show for its astonishing set, consisting of a series of intricately carved arches which Trevor Nunn had employed for his production of *Much Ado About Nothing* and were so costly that they had to do service for the Footlights as well.

Cambridge over, Graham Chapman went down to continue his medical studies at Bartholomew's Hospital, one of London's oldest teaching hospitals, where his brother had qualified.

The Footlights summer revue in the following year was the famous hard-to-

pronounce *A Clump of Plinths*, produced by Humphrey Barclay, which transferred to the West End as *Cambridge Circus*. When one of the cast, Tony Buffery, decided to drop out in order to pursue a professional career away from show-business, Graham Chapman was invited to take his place. The regime at Bart's was remarkably tolerant, and although the hours were long, evenings were a student's own. "By day I was doing medical clerking and surgical dressing, and by night I was falling around on stage – for about three months. That gave me a big taste for performing, I suppose." When the offer came to take the show to New Zealand he decided to take a year off from medicine and make the journey.

When he resumed his studies his other life in show-business had become both significant and lucrative. Cabaret appearances at the Blue Angel, contributions for radio and television, including *The Frost Report* followed, then an invitation came to write a series for Ronnie Corbett. "I'd qualified as a doctor and gone to Ibiza with John, and Marty Feldman was there. David Frost suddenly arrived, not even knowing where we were staying, and put all these proposals. It was a very exciting period."

The film was *The Rise and Rise of Michael Rimmer*, which was directed by Kevin Billington, and was about an efficiency expert who ascends eventually to become prime minister. Its release was delayed so long that by the time it finally appeared in 1970 Monty Python had also come upon the scene and rendered its style of comedy *passé*.

Graham Chapman had been anxious to acquire the letters MD after his name in case his show-business bubble was to burst. "I couldn't really see myself doing medicine for the rest of my life, however. It seemed too ordered, comfortable, protected. I wanted more adventure, some disruption in my life. I had an ear, nose and throat appointment lined up at Bart's which I threw up after I came back from Ibiza. I wrote for Roy Hudd, just to see if I could write on my own and not in partnership with John."

The fruits of his medical experience eventually helped to create the *Doctor* co-

medy series, under Humphrey Barclay's aegis at London Weekend. "John and I were contacted and we did the first episode, using my experience of first days at a hospital. It didn't take more than two or three days to write because it was all there in my head. From thereafter it was a very useful series for John and me. If one was ever short of a bit of loot one could go back and write a few episodes. I did about thirty, I think. It was a nice experience and certainly used up a backlog of medical stories."

The coming-together of the Pythons-to-be occurred with *The Frost Report* where the Cleese-Chapman writing partnership slowly got to know the Jones-Palin team. "I remember thinking 'Why does Terry Jones laugh so much?' They couldn't read out their material without laughing all the time. We weren't like that. What was interesting was that out of the twenty or so writers on *The Frost Report* the most prolific ones came together – Michael and Terry used to be very good at writing the bits of film that were used,

The Cambridge Circus *company. Graham Chapman is trouserless member of the chorus.*

Eric Idle was excellent at one-liners, and John and I used to then go in for a more verbal style of comedy – we realised that we all had something different to offer, and Barry Took brought us together with the idea of doing a series. Terry Gilliam I didn't know, but John did, and I think that he was responsible for bringing him into the group.

"We often felt when we were doing things for *The Frost Report* that some items that we knew were funny would not get done because it was felt that they were too rude or too silly. And with other people performing what we had written they also injected a lot of themselves into our material and changed it away from what we intended. We thought that apart from enjoying performing we would be able to do it how we wanted – we didn't have to worry about performers because we were going to do it ourselves. We could approach the thing as writers. We had much more control.

"I think that it was John who chose Sousa's *Liberty Bell* as our signature tune. He was always fascinated by Sousa. His musical tastes are not catholic. He likes Tijuana Brass and 'Simon Smith and the Amazing Dancing Bear' and that's about it. He doesn't even see the point of stereo."

Just as Terry Jones tended to let Michael Palin read out their material in script conferences, so it usually fell to John to present the Cleese-Chapman contributions. Initially there was a backlog of unused ideas from *The Frost Report* and many of them surfaced in the first Python series. Graham noted that it was generally fatal to present a piece of writing that demanded keen listening after lunch, while if it was a silly item then that was probably the best time. "Eric has the most difficult job since he's on his own – he doesn't have me or Terry Jones to giggle at his stuff."

All the Pythons were aware of the difference between Oxford and Cambridge attitudes. "We regarded the Oxford crowd as more emotional, and less logical in their thinking, while Cambridge people are more logical, and more hidebound in convention and practicalities. Cambridge people are keen to get out there, do it efficiently, earn some money and look professional. The Oxford ones have more heart, and get more emotionally involved. And they're possibly less self-critical. It's the icy cold winds of the Fens that makes Cambridge different."

He regards the present strength of Python as film-makers an outcome of the lack of pressure to stay together. The films happen because they want to do them, not because they must. He and John Cleese wrote two or three sketches based on biblical themes when they were at Cambridge, and found the progression to *The Life of Brian* easy, the screenplay falling together by the time they got to the sunny climate of Barbados. *The Meaning of Life* was harder, he believes, because they were pushed too soon to produce a final script, and by the time they went to the Caribbean they still had not got a good enough idea, with the consequence that the final film shows signs of hasty assembly, as well as being wasteful in material, much of which was excluded, not because it was not funny, but because its relevance was not apparent. He hopes that there will be a chance to use it in another context.

After completing *The Meaning of Life* he started work on *Yellowbeard*, a pirate spoof which he had written with Bernard McKenna and Peter Cook and had been attempting to make for several years. In the last week of filming on location in Mexico, Marty Feldman, who had a major part in the film, suffered a fatal heart attack. "It was terrible that it should have happened in Mexico City – there was a festival on and it took two hours for an ambulance to get through and take him to hospital and it was too late." Feldman was forty-nine.

Health is a primary concern of Graham Chapman, not merely because he is a doctor, but because he nearly died himself. He had begun to drink heavily at Cambridge, and eventually it reached an epic level. "It was awful, I was on three pints of gin a day, which is a lot. I came pretty close to snuffing. Because I withdrew myself with no medical attention, other than my own, I had three days in bed shivering and hallucinating – objects seemed to move like the way W.C. Fields shows it when he thinks something is lungeing at him when it isn't. Then after three days I stopped shaking and got up. But I hadn't eaten and I was very short of blood sugar. I went into muscular spasm, then an epileptic fit. When I came round I realised what a mess alcohol made of the body and that death was very close. That ended it.

"I enjoyed drinking a lot at first. It helped me because I was a quiet reserved person, rather shy. Alcohol does help where social intercourse is concerned. It became a crutch. I've been totally dry for five years now, and I wouldn't even take a chance with a glass of wine. I was affected by my own case, and also the death of a very close friend of mine, Keith Moon. He had had fits, too, and had actually bitten clean through his tongue. And yet, even after that he went back to drinking. I know it's a paradox that of all the Pythons I'm the one who knows the body most, and knows what the potential damage is, but oddly enough, I felt I could handle it – I'd take all the vitamin pills

and watch for the danger signs.

"I remember on the first day of filming *Holy Grail*, seven o'clock in the morning on a Scottish hillside, and nothing to drink – I suddenly had DTs. I was playing King Arthur in a cold drizzle, and I realised I was letting my friends down, and letting myself down. I stayed more or less on an even keel, not drinking too much, but I resolved to stop as soon as I could."

He wrote a semi-autobiography, called refreshingly enough *A Liar's Autobiography*, which while containing many hilarious and fantastically improbable anecdotes, is a not entirely untrue account of

WESTERN UNION
TELEGRAM
W. P. MARSHALL, PRESIDENT

CLASS OF SERVICE
This is a fast message
unless its deferred char-
acter is indicated by the
proper symbol.

SYMBOLS
DL=Day Letter
NL=Night Letter
LT=International Letter Telegram

57-1201 (4-60)

The filing time shown in the date line on domestic telegrams is LOCAL TIME at point of origin. Time of receipt is LOCAL TIME at point of destination

1964 OCT 28 PM 1 39

BZA079 BD224
B AMB101 PD FAX AM NEW YORK NY 28 1244P EDT
GRAHAM CHAPMAN, CARE HUMPHREY BARCLAY
CHESTERFIELD HOTEL
130 WEST 49 ST NYK
   REFERRING TO THE IMPENDING REOPENING OF CAMBRIDGE CIRCUS
AT SQUARE EAST, YOU ARE HEREBY NOTIFIED THAT AS AN EQUITY MEMBER
YOU ARE NOT PERMITTED TO PERFORM AT SQUARE EAST AS IT IS IN
VIOLATION OF SAFE AND SANITARY RULES. FURTHER, EQUITY WILL
NOT RELINQUISH ITS JURISDICTION OVER THIS PRODUCTION AND HAS
SO NOTIFIED AGVA. YOU ARE INSTRUCTED NOT TO REPORT TO THE THEATRE
NOR TO SIGN AGVA CONTRACTS FOR THIS PRODUCTION. EQUITY REMAINS
READY TO DISCUSS TERMS WITH MANAGEMENT
   ANGUS DUNCAN EXECUTIVE SECRETARY ACTORS EQUITY ASSN 226 WEST
47 ST NYC
(16).

his life up to that point. "It was as though I felt that that particular life is over, and I could write about it, and start afresh," he said. "It was like beginning a new life. For instance, I learned to drive at thirty-seven. I couldn't have done it previously."

His frankness about his alcoholism is partly due to a desire to help others, and by talking about it openly in the course of the launch of his book he gave some encouragement to other victims of the disease, although he has not belonged to Alcoholics Anonymous and, given his celebrity status, would find it somewhat difficult.

He is equally frank about his homosexuality. Some people have tried to link it with his drinking, but he firmly denies it. "I was an early campaigner for gay liberation. I realised some of the problems people had – I hadn't suffered them parti-

Cambridge Circus *on Broadway. A selection from Graham Chapman's personal album including 'One Man Wrestling', bottom left, and a Humphrey Barclay cartoon below.*

GRAHAM AS ARNOLD FITCH.

cularly, and the line of work I had opted for was probably the most tolerant towards that kind of behaviour – certainly medicine wasn't, which made me angry, because these were the people who should have been compassionate and understanding, and they were just being fascist as far as I could see. So that led to a kind of anger, which expressed itself in terms of buying tea urns for the Gay Liberation Front, and going to meetings, and wearing over-flowery trousers and generally being obnoxious to people in pubs. At one time my friends needed to protect me, I was such a danger. I remember being in a pub in Chalk Farm, and there had just been an England–Scotland football match. I was wearing the statutory flowery shirt and playing bar billiards when I heard a Glaswegian gentleman talking to his mate, say something about 'Jessie'. So I went over to him and said 'Why sneer at Jessies? I'm one', not quite knowing if I was going to get a bottle in my face. 'Look I'm a Jessie, I'm a homosexual.' There was a pause while he looked at me, then he said 'Och, that was fockin' brave. Let me buy ye a drink!' "

He had decided to give homosexuality a try at the age of twenty-five, having to that point been an uncertain hetero. "I was amazed at the similarity. The emotional relationships are slightly more intense, maybe because it's frowned upon by the rest of society. It didn't seem unnatural. It's something that very many people know about but pretend not to – they've indulged in it at school to an extent, not enough to make them homosexuals, but it does mean they know about it. The most important thing is that it's about being with someone with whom you click, someone you find physically and mentally attractive and you have a good time."

"I've always had a stable relationship going. David Sherlock with whom I have lived for sixteen years is still here, although we don't have a great deal going sexually now, because we've gone in slightly different directions, but that could happen to any married couple – we may come round together again, we may not. There are no rules for me, and I don't try to find any. But it does make me a bit of an outsider. And possibly I can observe others from a different standpoint which is useful. I don't necessarily accept what other people say as being the way things are in their relationships. What fascinated me in the beginning was not so much the difference, but the similarity. I'm not at all interested in procreation – I don't feel the need to reproduce myself around the earth, I don't know how I would feel if there was another little Chapman wandering around.

"There was no problem with the other Pythons when I told them. John was the only one who was very, very surprised and shocked. Marty just laughed. But they could have been amazed – after all, here was a pipe-smoking rugby player, keen on mountaineering. Jonathan Miller said I was a little unfair, presenting such a front to the world and then doing a turnaround. But I felt that the climate was right to come out, it was a cause I could do something for. I met Mrs Whitehouse (of the National Viewers and Listeners' Association) once and was surprised as most people are, and reasonably charmed by the lady. We talked about plants in Australia, nothing germane to the real nitty-gritty."

But it was Mrs Whitehouse who was instrumental in bringing a private prosecution against *Gay News*, a publication to which Graham Chapman had given financial support, for publishing a poem she considered blasphemous. While not liking the poem very much, he deplored her kind of censorship. He remembers taking part in a television chat show hosted by George Melly, and the conversation getting round to being gay. A woman viewer wrote in complaining that someone from Monty Python who did not have the courage to give his name (untrue) had confessed to homosexuality, and she enclosed a sheaf of prayers for the salvation of his soul, and quoted from the Bible "If a man lie with another he shall be taken out and killed." The letter ended up in the Python office, Eric Idle worked out a reply to the effect: "We have found out who it is and we've taken him out and killed him!"

Relaxing on the set of Life of Brian *with John Cleese.*

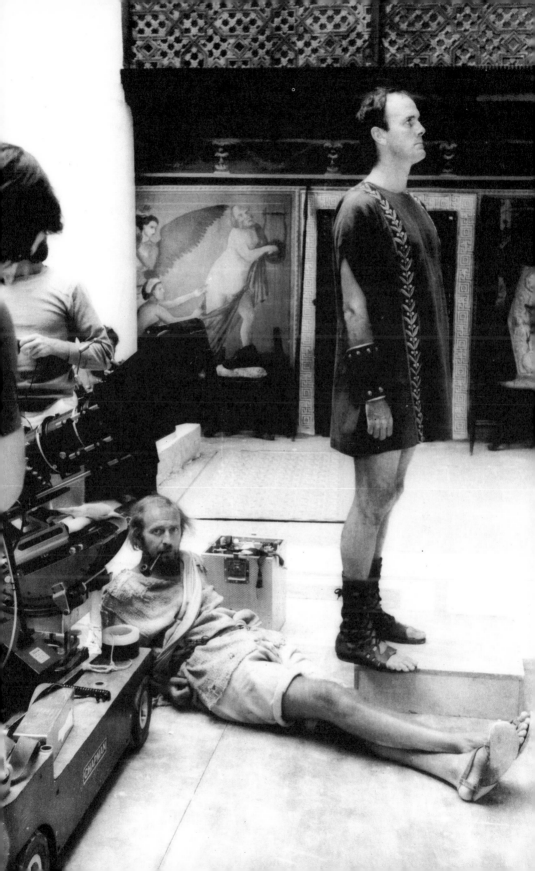

ERIC IDLE

IN ANY GROUP there is always one who walks alone, or so received opinion has it. Among the Pythons, Eric Idle has cast himself in that role. He has always found it easier to write by himself at his own pace, even though there have been times when he felt himself at a disadvantage when it came to presenting work to the others. Whereas Cleese and Palin could count on support from Chapman and Jones, and even Gilliam could get his own way by refusing to go into detail about his animations, Idle has had to make the running himself, and convince his colleagues that his material was funny. "It was easier with a show, because there were thirteen of them in a series, than it is with a film, where stuff is read out all the time, and you have got to convince five others. And they're not the most unegotistical of writers, either."

It's a handicap that has left him relatively unscathed. His worth as a member of the group is considerable. Not only can he create sparkling verbal humour in which ideas escalate into ever wilder fantasies, but he is an accomplished songwriter, and sharp parodist of many popular musical styles, an astringent performer with a special facility for grasping faultlessly tongue-twisting wordplays (in the business only Ronnie Barker excels him).

He came after everyone else at Cambridge. Graham Chapman had already gone down, John Cleese was in his final year, when he went up. He followed Graeme Garden and Tim Brooke-Taylor into the presidency of the Footlights Club, and went down in 1965.

Eric Idle was born in South Shields on 29 March, 1943. His father, who was serving in the Royal Air Force, was killed in a car crash when he was only two. "He died on Christmas Eve, which meant a bleak Christmas for my mother, at least." It also meant that the major part of his education took place at what he calls a semi-orphanage in the Midlands, an establishment which had earlier been attended by the novelist and poet Philip Oakes who has written a scathing and horrific account in his autobiography. By Idle's day the regime had softened a little, possibly he thinks because they had run out of orphans, but it was still very Victorian in atmosphere, with dormitories a hundred yards long.

He was there for twelve years from the age of seven onwards. Being one of the brighter pupils he maintained a steady academic progress, in spite of the distractions of nocturnal, illicit swimming sessions with girls from the school next door, and at eighteen decided to try for a place at Pembroke College, Cambridge. "I had to meet three people at the interview. One was an Arabic scholar, one was a professor of economics, and one was a mathematician. And I was going to read English, right? So we discussed what was on in the West End, which I happened to know – it was all we could talk about. Pembroke is a comedians' college, Peter Cook was there. I got through on the interview, I could never have passed the exams. It was odd, but to be encouraged, I think, that kind of selection. I'd never heard of the Footlights when I got there, but we had a tradition of college smoking-concerts, and I sent in some sketches parodying a play that had just been done. Tim Brooke-Taylor and Bill Oddie auditioned me for the Pembroke smoker, and that led to discovering about and getting into the Footlights, which was great. One could go and lunch in the clubroom, and swan in at about eleven at night and stay drinking until three. Lion's Yard was terrific, alas, all gone!"

The success of *Cambridge Circus* in the preceding year made it hard for the show that followed, *Stuff What Dreams are Made Of* and to his great disappointment, Eric Idle, although a contributor, was not selected by the director, Mark Lushington, to perform in it. The reviews were mild, and in any case his big opportunity came in the following year when he was made president of the club. The show for 1965 was called *My Girl Herbert*, and had a much stronger musical content than had been the case for some years, with John Cameron providing a pop-based score. There was also a reaction following the departure of John Cleese, whose long shadow had loomed heavily over Cambridge humour in Eric's first year. It was, in fact, a Cleese sketch called BBC BC in which an Old Testament prophet read the weather forecast, that Idle performed in his first Pembroke smoker, its author being ineligible to perform as he was not a member of the college. It was the first rendering of a famous *Cambridge Circus* item. "In fact John spent more time at Pembroke than at Downing. He used to dine at Pembroke nearly every night, and some of the dons actually thought that he was a Pembroke man. John was a very conservative figure in those days, wore tweed suits and belonged to the Pitt Club. He's always had that streak, half-caught by it, half-despising it. He's the closest thing to the English class system, he ought to be Sir John or Baron Cleese of Notting Hill."

Eric Idle's presidency of the Footlights coincided with the new spirit of liberation that swept across Britain in the mid-sixties, spearheaded by the eruption of pop music, especially that of the Beatles and the Rolling Stones, the mini-skirt, pop art and the curious phenomenon known as "swinging London". Harold Wilson's labour government came to power, and talk was of the white heat of technology and the new classlessness. Eric's contribution to this new Britain was to secure the full admission of women members in the Footlights. There had been occasional

breaks in the all-male tradition earlier. In 1932 a number of actresses had been imported to play in a musical comedy for May Week, called *Laughing at Love*, but its flop led to a reversion of policy and the following year's show was called *No More Women*. In 1957 two girls, Dorothy Mulcahy and Ann Jones, appeared in *Zounds*, written by Michael Frayn and John Edwards, and directed by Graeme McDonald. Two years later, Eleanor Bron appeared in John Bird's *The Last Laugh*. From then on most shows had one or two token women, including Jo Kendall, Miriam Margolyes and Felicity Hough, but they were there strictly by invitation, not as fully-fledged paid-up Footlights. Eric Idle bulldozed through the removal of this sexist barrier, and got four women in to the club who would appear in *My Girl Herbert*, among them an Australian postgraduate student at Newnham, Germaine Greer, who would later write *The Female Eunuch*. Among her most celebrated turns was a diverting striptease performed by a nun.

"Several of the gay dons were in tears when women came in, and they'd say things like 'Binky will simply die!' but me, in my little leather jacket at that stage, I was totally unsympathetic. Germaine came into the club at the same time as Clive James. She was a very funny lady. After getting out of the nun's habit she'd be down to a bikini and would put flippers on to go swimming. We toured England to various exotic locations such as Worcester and Ipswich, and we just limped near the West End for three patchy weeks at the Lyric Hammersmith with *My Girl Herbert*, a show only worth vaguely remembering.

"Then John Cameron and I went to The Blue Angel where we auditioned on a Saturday – it was a way they got a free cabaret when the place was packed. We took the place apart, we were wonderful. So we were booked for two weeks from the Monday. On the Monday night the audience was three Guards officers, two debs and eight bottles of champagne, and it's death for the rest of the week, not a titter. Then Richard Eyre did *Oh! What a Lovely War* at Leicester and called in all sorts of Cambridge people for it – it was an amazing production where every night the cast cried more than the audience – we were all so terrifically motivated – while they left for early buses. Then I got conned to stay for *One for the Pot*, which was possibly one of the worst parts ever written – I played a character who became notorious for not being on stage, because I would get so bored and be sitting in the dressing-room writing sketches, until one night an actor I was supposed to be on with came all the way up and said 'Would you mind joining me on stage?' I realised I didn't want to put up with being an actor. I was writing sketches for *I'm Sorry, I'll Read That Again* which they bought, and then for Frosty and *The Frost Report*." He joined the team, often supplying material for David Frost's Continuous Developing Monologue which had an escalatory style of absurdism that provided an excellent platform for his skills. It was the training ground for the Pythons, and the first opportunity of getting to know each other.

The next stage in his professional development was Humphrey Barclay's show for Rediffusion, *Do Not Adjust Your Set*, which brought him into contact with Neil Innes, then performing with the Bonzo Dog Band, and with whom he would later collaborate on *The Rutles*. Terry Jones and Michael Palin were also part of the team and David Jason and Denise Coffey formed the non-Oxbridge element. It was a show primarily aimed at children, and shown in the late afternoon-early evening viewing period for such programmes, but rapidly achieved a cult following among adults, who would rush home early to catch it. A second series followed, although the contractor had now become Thames, Rediffusion having been absorbed following the shake-up of Independent Television. He then went on to another Humphrey Barclay show, hosted by Frank Muir, called *We Have Ways of Making You Laugh*, which was mostly the improvised musings of a resident panel, but with sketches and appearances from Eric. Terry Gilliam had drifted into the show as a cartoonist, and found Eric was relatively nice to him in spite of his bizarre appearance and transatlantic accent. When Barry Took assembled the team for the series that was to become *Monty Py-*

Left, *Eric Idle in Footlights, 1964.* Below, *On tour with the Footlights 1965, in* My Girl Herbert. *John Cameron at the piano, Clive James standing behind Eric Idle.*

thon's Flying Circus, Gilliam was included at Eric Idle's urging.

Ironically, in the structure of the group, just as Terry Jones represented the opposite end of the spectrum to John Cleese, it was Terry Gilliam who stood in most contrast to Eric Idle. The Idle wit is razor-sharp, intellectually based, logically formed. By contrast, Gilliam is wild and anarchic, zany and earthy, with a scatological streak. As the two lone rangers of the group it is perhaps natural the search for polarities should end up on them. When the Pythons approved the decision to produce a book based on the success of the television series it was a project that fell directly under Eric's wing, with scant help from Gilliam who felt that he had exhausted the scissors-and-paste drudgery of layout during his days on a humorous magazine. " 'Funny books don't sell,' said Terry and he wouldn't ever discuss it. We had to raid his house and steal old bits of his cutouts." Eric brought in an outside designer, Derek Birdsall, to art direct *Monty Python's Big Red Book*. The Idle method of editing was to closet himself with the material and his designer, Birdsall, or Kate Hepburn, not emerging until a satisfactory dummy had been produced. Intensive methods worked, and the books have generated a satisfactory ancillary income for the group, thanks to Eric's drive and editorial skill, sometimes in the face of apathy from the other Pythons.

When John Cleese broke the knot and departed after the third series, Eric, too felt that he would like to branch out on his own, and after the fourth was completed he persuaded the BBC to run *Rutland Weekend Television*, a weekly half-hour for BBC2 which carried the technique of television parody to its ultimate, purporting to be the programme output of Britain's smallest independent station. The budget was so low that the ramshackle appearance of its presentation was scarcely satirical, but the byproduct of BBC parsimony. The whole thing was staged in a tiny studio too small to admit an audience, with Eric Idle in the guise of announcer introducing studio interviews and filmed inserts. Neil Innes supplied some of the musical items, including parodies or pastiches of popular songs and it

was from this series that the idea for *The Rutles* was eventually to emerge. RWT had two seasons, in 1975 and the following year. A sequence by Neil Innes was used in the NBC show *Saturday Night Live* in 1977, during a temporary hosting stint by Eric, which featured a bogus group singing a number in the style of the Beatles. The brief appearance of "The Rutles" caused a minor sensation, and NBC suggested a full-length biography of the imaginary group be made, and advanced the money and facilities. Innes and Idle set to work writing a number of pastiche songs and filming took place in England, using a documentary technique, including mock vox-pop interviews with unnamed celebrities such as Mick Jagger and Paul Simon. George Harrison, a genuine Beatle, played a journalist conducting an interview with Michael Palin. *The Rutles* followed the Beatles story very closely, exposing the shortcomings of the media as much as the mismanagement of the group, and was rich in accurately observed detail, including the use of archive footage to evoke the correct atmosphere. The devotion to the parody form even extended to the subsequent album sleeve which mimicked several of The Beatles' most famous records. Neil Innes provided music of a high standard, accurately capturing the

Do Not Adjust Your Set cast. Eric Idle, Michael Palin, Terry Jones, David Jason and Denise Coffey.

wistful poignancy of McCartney in *The Fool on the Pill* for instance, and the work still stands as the best and most affectionate attempt to imitate the most famous pop group of all time. On the strength of his brilliant work Neil Innes was given his own BBC series *The Innes Book of Records* in which he was able to perform his idiosyncratic songs in atmospheric and often surrealist settings.

Eric Idle's friendship with George Harrison also pulled the entire Monty Python team out of trouble when EMI cancelled its backing for *The Life of Brian*. Through his intervention and backing the film went ahead and HandMade Films started up in business.

In common with the other Pythons Idle regards the films as the fruitful and logical direction they should take, rather than television. "When I look at the *Fringe* group, Peter Cook and the others, and see they're not together, I can see the value in having to lose your ego like us, and come together and suffer a little and produce work – it's actually reassuring as you get older. The older John gets, the more it will be pleasant for him to realise that he isn't just a loony – there are five other loonies with him, and we can't all be completely mad if we agree. Comedy is something where you suffer for other people – there's something involved in being up to your neck in muck which makes people laugh. John is wonderful, he's enormously talented and funny, has a tremendously bleak view of life, and he isn't going to be remembered by posterity for his Sony commercials. He needs to have his rear end kicked sometimes to produce this kind of work, even if it means roughing it. We are all supercritical about each other – the day we say 'Wonderful, darling!' and become like Richard Attenborough we're sunk. I think it's the important thing – we do all keep a strong critical eye on what everyone else is doing. It's healthy, and if you're reading scripts out to everyone and something doesn't work, it's better to get that sort of criticism while you're still making the film than when it is out – at least you have a chance to make it better."

The Python's frankness about one another is an unusual manifestation in a business renowned for the gushing bonhomie exhibited to the public when in reality the knives are drawn. Whatever disagreements occur there's a basic respect for each other as colleagues. Eric is criticised by the others for remaining aloof from the nuts and bolts of film-making. As soon as *The Meaning of Life* had finished he was off making *Yellowbeard*, and then wintered in Australia during the frantic period in which Terry Jones was trying to achieve a final cut. Graham Chapman was similarly castigated, although to be fair, there comes a time on any film when the director is the only person for whom it is appropriate to make a

creative decision. "Terry Jones constantly changes his mind on tiny details. To be around watching minor changes is a totally frustrating experience," says Eric. "Towards the end he is much more in need of support and a fresh eye, hence I thought to stay away and come home in March. The advancing of the deadline meant that instead of coming in at the right time I could see the rough cut only on video in Sydney. I still feel that what I saw there was better than the final cut."

Rutland Weekend Television gave viewers beauty queens, accountancy shanties and the world-famous 'Rutles'.

Eric vividly remembers the occasion when Graham Chapman revealed to the others what he got up to in the evenings. "I didn't know even when I was writing with him. He was leading an incredible double life. He had this wonderful party where he decided to tell everybody. It was a very interesting evening. For a long time, I think because of the alcohol, we never got on, we were close to fighting a lot of the time. Since he became sober that ceased to happen. Anyway, I remember at that party he suddenly said, 'I want you all to meet the man I love', and I knew at once that it wasn't a joke, that he was deadly serious. Marty Feldman was very good about it, but there was a girl there who was in love with him who was weeping, she was absolutely distraught. Marty, who was then our script editor, said that we weren't to stop making pouf jokes, that it shouldn't make any difference. He was right of course; if you're working with someone their sex life isn't what counts, it's the quality of their ideas, what they can offer. But writing teams are like marriages, they go through their moods and break up – Marty and Barry Took, Michael and Terry, Graham and John."

While shunning the scriptwriting partnership as much as possible, he has had two shots of marriage itself, the first to an Australian actress in 1969, Lyn Ashley, from whom he was divorced in 1975. His son Carey was born in 1973. He married again in 1981, but can't actually remember the date, pursuing a theory that men never remember the date they get married the second time. His wife Tania is an American model he met in New York during the days of *Saturday Night Live*. Another of his theories is that Englishmen should never marry English women as they make the wrong kind of noises together. "Tania's a perfect American – her mother's Italian and her father's Russian! She's not in show-business, she is not impressed by it. She's rarely interested in what I write – eventually I'll force her to read something. She's perfectly normal, balanced and sane. She's lovely, what more can I say?"

It befits his cosmopolitan attitude. In London he lives in St John's Wood, close enough to the Lords cricket ground to watch his favourite sport, but for much of the year he stays away. Another of his theories is that the nicest, most interesting British people don't live in their homeland. "I really appreciate England when I'm travelling around the world. The best Englishmen are the expatriates – they're wonderful people. This is a small island. The options after you have done a series of your own are not that open – you go from BBC2 to BBC1 to ITV, that's it. I think it's more challenging to keep moving. I like working with people who are good – I think that Python are much the best in this country, probably the best, and I like to meet people who are that serious about their business in other parts of the world.

"I'm very fond of stars – I like looking at the sky. I'm very fond of warm weather and I like swimming. Writing is such a sedentary, debilitating experience that I like to exercise. Outside of Python what interests me is doing things I haven't done before. In England I try very hard. I wrote a play because I thought the West End was dying on its feet – all these empty theatres and the best actors unemployed. I wrote a play (*Pass the Butler*) which was a very interesting and enjoyable experience, until it came into the West End when we were shat upon from a great height. If I did a play now I wouldn't even bring it into the West End. I would just tour England with it. Coming in is so prohibitive, so expensive, that you are much better off taking plays round where people can see them more easily. I'll always love the theatre for giving me my first break. *Beyond the Fringe* was a big moment for me. Everyone talks about the Goons – but the Goons didn't mean that much to me. However, when I saw *Beyond the Fringe*, that was it, it was so very, very funny about taboo subjects.

"The Goons came from radio and tried to adapt their stuff to television and that was difficult. We Pythons didn't have that obsession – we were writing for television and could see the potential for what you could do with it. We were the first people really, after TW3 to play with the toys. And when we had exhausted what we could do with television we started to explore film."

MONTY PYTHON

THERE ARE CONFLICTING theories as to how the name *Monty Python's Flying Circus* came to be adopted. The Cambridge element were all for calling the show *Owl-Stretching Time*. Another candidate was a football team's forward line invented by Cleese, called *Bunn, Wackett, Buzzard, Stubble and Boot*. Barry Took recalls a meeting with Michael Mills, head of comedy at the BBC, who told the assembled executives: "When Took requests something you realise that he's really giving you an order, just like Baron von Richthofen. Or Baron von Took." It was but a short step towards the project becoming known as Baron von Took's Flying Circus, after the celebrated German aviator of the First World War, and it was thus designated on memos, eventually abbreviated to the Flying Circus. But there are those who suspect that *Cambridge Circus* had something to do with it, in view of the earlier associations. Having got thus far, Michael Palin happened to spot the name Gwen Dibley in a local newspaper, and for a while the show was to be *Gwen Dibley's Flying Circus*. Then out of discussion the name Monty, representing a shady sort of theatrical booker, the sort of man who fixes a fourth-rate act up with a week at Workington, and Python as an unlikely surname, were gloriously combined, producing an octosyllabic title of pleasant resonance. It also put paid to a proposal to give the show a new title each week, an idea that the BBC had viewed with horror and disbelief.

Eric Idle proposed that Terry Gilliam be brought into the group to provide a unifying graphic style, starting with the credit titles, which would be constructed from his animated collage technique. Gilliam's writhing tendrils, dancing heads and distinctive lettering were orchestrated to the wonderfully appropriate strains of Sousa's march, *Liberty Bell*, a happy choice of signature tune that has since rendered it difficult for the band of the Grenadier Guards to include in their repertoire at Buckingham Palace without provoking amusement from the watching crowd. The titles terminated with a large foot squelching through the frame from above, accompanied by a raspberry sound effect.

Gilliam's most important role was to be in the creation of animation links, which in themselves were so surrealistic, absurd and unpredictable that they could lead in any direction. The free-form style was to influence the character of the show itself, which abandoned the notion of a fixed framework. "I remember," said Terry Jones, "watching *Q5*, Spike Milligan's show on BBC2, and thinking 'He's done it!' He'd got it all – scenery being pushed off the set in mid-sentence, sketches abandoned in the middle and completely new ones taking over. Spike was doing what we wanted to do. We'd all been writing cliches – sketches with beginnings, middles and ends – and suddenly there was Milligan doing this amazing stuff. I remembered an elephant animation Terry Gilliam had done for *Do Not Adjust Your Set* – it was a sort of stream-of-consciousness of disconnected images, using Terry's stuff to link them all together. Milligan had shown us how you could end sketches in the middle without it really mattering – so I talked to Mike Palin about it. The three of us felt that this was the shape, the right thing. But it was a bit of a fight when we started into the shows. John tolerated the idea, but felt that it was the sketches that mattered."

John Howard Davies was the producer and director of the first four Monty Python programmes, then Ian McNaughton directed thereafter. McNaughton had been the director of Milligan's *Q5*, which had shown Terry Jones the light, and he fell easily into the Monty Python established style when the first programmes were recorded.

The first *Monty Python's Flying Circus* went out on 5 October, 1969, a Sunday, and appeared in a slot hitherto filled by a repeat of a religious discussion that had taken place earlier in the evening. As a result of sagging ratings it had been decided to drop it in favour of entertainment, a move that was criticised by those who still adhered to the Reithian view that Sundays were only for uplift and enlightenment. Appropriately, the Pythons introduced themselves with their new catchphrase, itself mocking the conventions of BBC continuity announcers: "And now for Something Completely Different". John Cleese would usually

Spike Milligan with John Bluthal in his show Q5 (followed by Q6, 7, 8 and 9) heavily influencing early Python thinking.

utter it while seated at a desk in some unlikely location – a seashore, the middle of a field, or a lake. The shows were not transmitted in the order in which they were recorded, but shuffled around to ensure that the strongest appeared first and last in the run. In fact, the programme that was recorded first went out in the second week, and included such Python favourites as "It's the Arts", a take-off of a TV programme in which John Cleese played an interviewer obsessed with how he should address his distinguished guest instead of getting on with it, and the funniest joke in the world, a gagline of such potency that it causes its writer to die laughing, which is then translated into German and used as a secret weapon in the Second World War against the Nazis, who it seems were working on their own joke when they were defeated in 1945. The first programme to be transmitted included Arthur Ewing and his musical mice, a Terry Jones character who plays *The Bells of St Mary's* by striking each of the unfortunate (and happily, unseen animals) with a mallet; the marriage guidance counsellor sketch in which Michael Palin and Carol Cleveland (who became the stock pretty female in the Python shows – most women being played by the others

in drag) visit Eric Idle for advice, only to have him make a heavy, reciprocated pass at her; and a parody of *The World Around Us* which was about men and mice, famous men who have been mice, and men who dress as mice, squeak and eat cheese.

Parodies of television shows were a stock item of Python humour, not in itself particularly original, but because they offered opportunities to plumb the depths of the absurd within a framework that was recognisable and respectable (as well as parading madmen and freaks before po-faced anchormen, or often where the interviewer was the insane party) it was possible to mock the very essence of television. A quiz show parody with Mao, Lenin, Karl Marx and Che Guevara eagerly competing to answer questions on English football teams, for instance, aptly caught the mind-numbing inanity of such shows.

"Much of Python comedy is simple reversal," says Barry Took. "Take Hell's Grannies. That's straight out of the Child's Book of How to Write Comedy. Thugs beating up old ladies? Why not

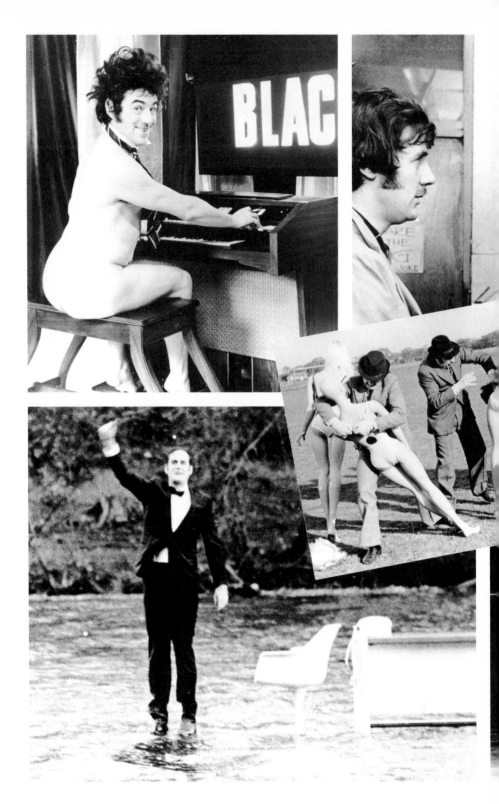

have old ladies ganging up, roaming the streets looking for thugs to bash, young people to bully? But it's the way they do it that's so good."

Another Python staple is the type of sketch in which an interviewer sits in an office and deals with a visitor. A vocational guidance counsellor faces an accountant who wants to be a liontamer. A distinguished explorer with double vision asks a candidate whom he insists on addressing in the plural to climb a twin-peaked mountain. The classic of the genre is the one where the man at the desk conducts an argument for a fee.

It was Michael Palin and Terry Jones who lobbied at the start for plenty of filmed sequences, which Ian McNaughton directed even before he was responsible for the whole show. Most comedy programmes made by BBC television did their filming in the adjacent Home Counties, often straying no further than the streets of Acton and Shepherds Bush because they were near the studios, but Python broke away and took the cameras to wild, uninhabited sections of the Yorkshire moors and Scottish highlands, subjecting all the personnel involved to considerable discomfort, yet producing superb footage. For the first series Michael Palin evolved a strange hair-shirted figure called The Hermit. This shaggy, dirt-covered creature would haul himself into view in some remote landscape and after dodging a series of improbable hazards would crawl towards the camera and gasp "It's.....!" before collapsing, as Terry Gilliam's opening-title animation would take over and someone else, usually Cleese, would announce "Monty Python's Flying Circus!" and *Liberty Bell* would strike up.

Part of Python's televisual preoccupation would show in the way they dealt with titles. Programme credits would sometimes appear in the middle of the show, or even at the beginning. They

Python classics. Clockwise from top left; Terry Jones as Blackmail's organist; Michael Palin and John Cleese with "this 'ere parrot"; Hell's Grannies on the rampage; John Cleese about to make the announcement and centre, in the race for 'Upper Class Twit of the Year'.

129

would be in the form of anagrams (following an Eric Idle interview as a man who spoke only in anagrams, and was working on an anagram version of *Hamlet*: "Thamel ... be ot or bot neot, tath is the nestoqui", or in mock-German or bogus Scandinavian, or even sign language. Even as the last credit had rolled together with the copyright line, there might still be a hanging gag, making it difficult for the continuity staff to adjust things for the succeeding programme. The BBC1 logo, a rotating globe against a distorted reflection of itself, was frequently used in a scurrilous manner, and the solemnities of BBC News presentation were constantly mocked. Ten years later the *Not the Nine O'Clock News* show carried this style of comedy to its logical conclusion.

Various stock figures evolved. The most prominent were a band of strident, domineering, middle-aged women known to the group as Pepperpots on account of the shape of their bodies. It was such

ladies (the Pythons have always excelled in drag) who in the guise of the Batley Townswomen's Guild would re-enact the battle of Pearl Harbor in mud. Their masculine counterparts were the Gumbies, a group of lower-middle class men who wore gumboots, trousers rolled above their knees, fair isle pullovers over white shirts with the sleeves rolled up, and white handkerchiefs on their heads, each corner knotted. The original of this character, reflecting some atavistic memory of a prewar filing clerk on the beach at Margate, was created by Michael Palin and quickly cloned by the others.

Graham Chapman, the tall (although not as tall as John Cleese) pipe-smoking reasonable man, invented a bristling, indignant colonel in uniform, who would sometimes stride into the middle of sketches and demand that they be terminated on the grounds that they were silly. Another method for abruptly terminating unpromising material was simply to drop

a 16-ton weight on to the offender. Cleese became famous, if not notorious, for his absurd civil service department, the Ministry of Silly Walks. Terry Jones, small, dark, voluble and Welsh, was particularly adept at playing shrill women. But one of his more bizarre characterisations was the naked, smirking organist, first seen introducing an audience participation show called *Blackmail*.

The most celebrated sketch in the first series was the one involving a pet shop proprietor (Palin) and an indignant customer (Cleese) complaining that he had been sold a dead parrot, an assertion discounted with increasing desperation by the proprietor, leading to an escalating outpour of protest from the aggrieved party, culminating with the lines:

"This parrot is no more. It has ceased to be. It's expired and gone to meet its maker. This is a late parrot. It's a stiff. Bereft of life it rests in peace. If you hadn't nailed it to its perch it would be pushing up daisies. It's rung down the curtain and joined the choir invisible! *This is an ex-parrot!*"

It was to become probably the most famous of all Python situations, although in view of the simple two-handed interchange involved at the time it looked no different from many similar ones.

For the first time all the participants experienced the benefits of being left to get on with it – interference from the BBC hierarchy was initially minimal at script level. Although Hugh Greene had left the director-generalship in April 1969 his influence was still to persist for a while, and Huw Wheldon, then television's managing director, was at pains to see that judgments were supported, not sabotaged. The biggest complaint the Pythons had in the first series was that the time of transmission was not constant, sometimes even

John Cleese in formal Civil Service attire demonstrates the complete silly walk. (Warning: do not attempt this yourself, it is dangerous).

jumping a week if sporting events and other occasions squeezed it out, and such timetable quirks were making it difficult to establish a regular audience. Nevertheless, they were able to elevate their ratings from a reasonable one million to an excellent three million, and there was no hesitation from the Corporation over the commissioning of a second series. It was also decided that the budget would be increased, and that the transmission slot would be fixed. It proved a dubious advantage when it was found that the hour chosen, after 10 pm, was the time when the BBC regions opted for their own programmes and switched away from the network, with the result that apart from London and the North no other part of the country saw it the first time around, and had to wait for rescheduling.

Most television critics after a six-week silence were captivated by Python. Stanley Reynolds in *The Times*, for instance, said that it would "Still be an incredible bargain to the BBC at twice the price."

The six Pythons were augmented by Carol Cleveland, who played the pretty girl parts. The inner ring of the circular BBC Television Centre formed an apt setting for a first series publicity picture. Above, All the Pythons in one sketch for a 'How to Hit People over the Head' demonstration.

There were one or two dissenters. Milton Shulman in the London *Evening Standard* wrote: "The chief fault of *Monty Python's Flying Circus* is that it occasionally reveals an inability to recognise a good joke from a bad one and will stretch unpromising ideas to almost unbearable limits." Virginia Ironside in the *Daily Mail* was perturbed by the tendency to abort sketches for "being silly" before they had time to reach a punchline, saying: "I have always sat through the show with a distinct sneer playing round my mouth."

Connoisseurs of Python tend to regard the second series as reflecting the team at its peak as far as television is concerned. It is a view held by some of the members themselves. The level of invention is extremely high, and there is an air of great confidence. Silly walks appeared in the first show broadcast in the new series (but not the first recorded) as did Terry Gilliam's fearsome hedgehog, Spiny Norman. The Spanish Inquisition, a disconnected sketch in which a trio of robed clerics (Palin, Gilliam and Jones as Cardinal Biggles with goggles) exploded into incongruous settings and attempted to torture Carol Cleveland with a dish-drying rack, was a highlight of the second programme. Other joys included the At-

Above, *The finger of God (actually Gilliam) points to Eric Idle, a miscreant in the 'Salvation Fuzz' sketch.* Below, *The 'Dirty Vicar' sketch in which Terry Jones played the lascivious Rev Ronald Sims allegedly won the Mountbatten Trophy for the dirtiest television item.*

tila the Hun Show and How to Recognise Different Parts of the Body. A famous sketch allegedly set in the philosophy department of an Australian university suggested that the faculty lived only on beer and were all called Bruce. A semaphore version of *Wuthering Heights* was another agreeable absurdity.

By 1970 the effects of a new regime were being felt at the BBC. During Hugh Greene's era as Director-General a pressure group called the National Viewers and Listeners' Association had been formed on Moral Majority lines, to counteract the spread of permissiveness in television. Its vigorous spokeswoman and secretary, Mrs Mary Whitehouse, was an ex-schoolteacher who, largely as a result of an instinctive talent for engineering press publicity, became a national celebrity, and the bane of Greene's life. Liberalisation came to an end after his departure, and *Monty Python* was subjected to Whitehousian wrath in spite of the lateness of the hour at which it was transmitted. Particular exception was taken to a sketch in the last show of the second series in which John Cleese takes his dead mother in a sack to an undertaker, played by Graham Chapman, who after a lengthy conversation on alternative methods of interment suggests cooking and eating her with french fries, broccoli and parsnips. It was clearly black humour, and likely to be offensive to anyone who could not see it as such. Even some of the Pythons were somewhat doubtful as to whether they would get away with it, particularly Terry Jones and Michael Palin. But it was performed, although Michael Mills, the head of Comedy, who on this occasion had been consulted by Ian McNaughton, requested that the audience should show its disapproval by rushing on to the set, a somewhat contrived pay-off. When that show has been repeated the item has been omitted, although the Pythons have performed it on stage.

"We were all very polite to one another during the first series," recalls Michael Palin, "we all submerged our idiosyncrasies for the general good of the show, but that wore off during the second series." The Python method, by which material would be presented and voted on for inclusion or rejection had advantages and drawbacks, with two writing duos, Cleese and Chapman, Palin and Jones, and two loners, Idle and Gilliam, whose contribution was not one in which other members could usefully collaborate. Gilliam had the edge on the others in that his animations were usually not ready at that stage and had to be accepted on trust, to the occasional annoyance of John Cleese in particular, who liked to see the niceties of the democratic process observed. "As a general rule, the largest parts tended to be taken by the people who had written them," said Palin. "How I could have written such an uncomfortable role as the hermit, I'll never know."

After the second series the Pythons were assembled for their hastily produced cinema film called *And Now for Something Completely Different*. It was nothing of the sort, merely an anthology of some of the more successful items from the first two series reshot on 35 mm film in a widescreen format. The team worked for five weeks on various locations, with the bulk of the interiors filmed in an improvised studio at a former dairy milk depot in north London. The parrot sketch, *Blackmail*, the Lumberjack Song in which a

The 'Summarize Proust' competition, apart from causing tremors within the BBC led on to ways of attacking Belgians (the legs are Carol Cleveland) and later in the same show the meeting of the two sons of a woman played by Terry Jones, the dusky Eamonn (Graham Chapman), just in from Belfast, and Mervyn (John Cleese) who has been trying to summon the fire brigade.

1972
SUMMARIZE
PROUST
COMPETITION

7 THE PAST RECAPTURED
6 THE SWEET CHEAR GONE
5 THE CAPTIVE
4 CITIES OF THE PLAIN
3 THE GUERMANTES WAY
2 WITHIN A BUDDING GROVE
1 SWANN'S WAY

Gumby Michael Palin calls on a Gumby Harley Street surgeon (John Cleese) who decides to carry out a brain removal with his Gumby team.

chorus of Canadian mounties discover in succeeding verses that the rugged hero is a transvestite, Pearl Harbor in mud, the funniest joke in the world, killer cars, hell's grannies, man with a tape recorder up his nose and the Upper Class Twit of the Year contest were among the old favourites that were included. The producer of the film, Victor Lownes, then ran the Playboy Club in London, which at the time was the most profitable of Hugh Hefner's establishments on account of its gambling. It was Lownes' intention to introduce the Pythons to a new audience in the United States, and he expected the film to be successful on the college circuit. He demanded, much to Terry Gilliam's annoyance, a large credit, apparently carved out of stone, in the middle of the title animation, and he also exercised control on what items should be included, leaving, as Michael Palin put it, "too many people sitting behind desks". In spite of an extra polish given to many of the sketches over their television counterparts, the film is indigestible, there being far too much in it to sustain the audience's attention over the timespan of feature-length running time. The Pythons do not look back on it with any great affection and don't like it to be compared with their subsequent films, which they made themselves. "There were a number of very good performances," said Palin, "but un-

fortunately it doesn't expand on to the big screen very well. You can get away with very tatty sets on telly - it's all part of it - but you can't do the same apologies for quality on film." It was not a success in America as the Pythons meant nothing at that time to the audience at which it was aimed, but being a low-budget work (a mere £80,000) it easily went into profit on its British release, although the team saw little if anything in financial returns for themselves.

By now the Pythons were beginning to appreciate that they had an intrinsic commercial value as a group. They had made a record album of the first series for the BBC but were not wholly satisfied with the way it was produced. By forming Python Productions they set up the machinery to retain full artistic control (and profits) of their various enterprises, which included further record albums and books. *Monty Python's Big Red Book* was published in time for Christmas 1971 (it had, as it so happened, a very assertive blue cover) and consisted of a collage of absurdity, some of it derived from the show itself (such as a photostrip of Cleese doing a Silly Walk, lyrics of the Lumberjack Song, a spoof Radio Times piece on

In another show Eric Idle, wearing a shoddy toupee, is confronted by a batch of shoddily-toupeed toupee salesmen (note the toupeed portrait of Ian Paisley).

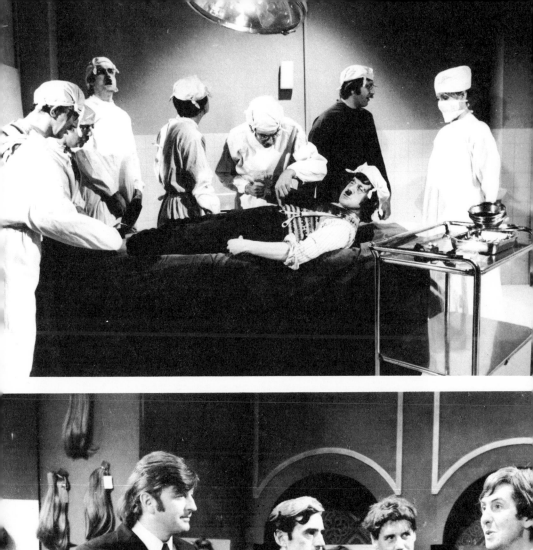

the Upper Class Twit of the Year) but the bulk of it was original material expertly assembled by Eric Idle. A resourceful publisher, Geoffrey Strachan at Methuen, not only saw immediately the excellent market that could be opened up for the book, but also helped to pioneer spinoffs from other television comedy shows in book publishing. The *Big Red Book* was followed by *The Brand New Monty Python Bok*, a title that was to challenge those who have made a career from typesetting, and it reappeared in a softback edition as *The Brand New Monty Python Papperbok*. The white cover carried some very realistic inky thumbsmears, and caused intense irritation at bookshops throughout the country from customers who had been taken in by the joke. The second book, again compiled by Idle, had very little television-derived material (an exception is a picture story on *Salad Days* as directed by Sam Peckinpah) but there was a great deal of ambitious special printing in the form of inserts and tip-ins, including a parody of a Penguin paperback.

In April 1971, in the face of some opposition feeling that it was an inappropriate choice, the BBC entry at the Montreux Television Festival was a *Monty Python* special compiled from several shows, and it won the Silver Rose. The honour helped to secure a third series, but the BBC Handbook for 1972 merely lists the award alongside various other accolades picked up in the course of the year, and makes no other editorial reference. Although the recordings for the third series began in December, they were not on the air until the following October. Tensions within the group were increasing, and John Cleese, who had become the best-known of the Pythons (truck drivers spotting him on the street would call upon him to do a silly walk there and then) was extremely restless. He felt that many of their ideas were being regurgitated. "I have an extremely low boredom threshold," Cleese admits. "They wanted to hang on because they were enjoying it. I wanted to get away and do other things. I wasn't keen to do the third series, but I agreed to do seven, and was somehow pressured into doing thirteen. I found by that time we were repeating ourselves, and

Chapman and Jones as 'Come Dancing' fanatics Gladys and George, settle down to watch a television documentary on molluscs. Right, John Cleese as Ann Elk attempts to tell interviewer Graham Chapman her Brontosaurus Theory. Below right, Queen Victoria, accompanied by a coffin containing her late husband, discusses ants with sundry 19th-century poets.

that the sketches we were writing were a combination of old ones. I could literally look at those sketches in the third series and say that this item was a combination of this sketch from the first, and that from the second, with a twist on it. I wasn't getting much pleasure out of it."

His increasing twitchiness was viewed with resentment by the rest of the group. Cleese recalls: "The ones who were most vitriolic – and a couple were very rude about it, although I didn't realise it for a time – were the ones who were most threatened because they weren't confident that they could earn a living outside the group. They were Terry Jones and Graham. Michael was the nearest to me in many ways — I don't think he was that bothered by the thought, and was happy to go off and do other things. I think Terry Gilliam was split both ways. I think that he wanted to go off, but probably didn't feel quite confident enough to. And I think that Eric wasn't all that bothered, either – I think he felt like taking a risk. But Terry Jones has always felt frightened at operating outside the group – yet he's got masses of talent, masses!"

Terry Jones agrees that in 1973 he had less going outside Python than some of the others, and was unhappy about the

Top, *Eric Idle confronts shopkeeper John Cleese and annoys him by talking only in verse.* Centre, *A fourth series sketch in which Mr and Mrs Zambesi are equipped with artificial brains.* Bottom, *More Hit-on-the-Head lessons from Graham Chapman, making an arrest under the Strange Sketch Act.* Right, *One of the standard methods of aborting overlong sketches – the dread 16-ton weight, about to flatten John Cleese.*

departure of John. "I don't think I was vitriolic, though. I understood why John wanted to go. It's true that we'd all thrown a lot into Python, but I don't think I was as angry as John imagines."

There had been signs in the third series of a hardening line. The BBC was becoming concerned that sections of its audience found *Monty Python* offensive, and vociferous groups such as the Festival of Light and Mrs Whitehouse's National Viewers and Listeners' Association were constantly lobbying the BBC's new chairman, Lord Hill. He had been switched to that job from a similar position at ITV by the Prime Minister, Harold Wilson, as a blatant act of revenge, following a number of incidents which suggested that the Corporation was not exactly on the side of his government. Hill had seen Hugh Carleton-Greene off, and Wilson lost the 1970 general election to the Conservatives under Edward Heath. Heath, however, kept Hill at the BBC. During the third Python series the group found themselves under threat of censorship. "We had been very spoiled," says Michael Palin, "and we had really done what we liked." They had acquired a following in Germany, having produced one show for Bavarian television in which they had spoken their lines phonetically. Their second show was to be a compilation of items from the BBC series, but the Pythons were not keen to do this and proposed to stage a complete programme directed by Ian McNaughton in the Munich studios. McNaughton was sent a letter listing "Thirty-two Points of Worry" based on a scrutiny of all the programmes by Bill Cotton, the head of light entertainment, and Duncan Wood, head of comedy. McNaughton returned from Germany and he and the Pythons attended a meeting to be told that words like "masturbation" were not to be used in comedy shows. They claimed that some of the objections revealed more about the objectors than themselves, pointing out that their would-be censors could not tell the difference between a severed arm and a giant penis. Eventually cuts were agreed, though on a much smaller scale than those originally demanded.

A sketch that had caused some trouble was the *Summarise Proust Competition*, a

spoof TV contest in which contestants had to offer 15-second synopses of all the novels forming *A La Récherche du Temps Perdu*. Graham Chapman, on being asked his hobbies, had said "Golf, strangling animals and masturbation," but the BBC removed the last word from the audio track, although he is clearly seen mouthing it. In vain was it protested that the lateness of the hour of transmission should ensure that those who were corruptible would have been long in bed.

By using shock effects such as severed limbs and simulated rape the Pythons were extending the bounds of humour. Their literacy put them on a different plane from the smutty comedians in men's clubs. In many respects they were commenting on and mocking the very permissiveness for which they were thought to

be crusading. Sketches such as Pasolini's *Third Test Match*, or in the same programme those aimed at Oscar Wilde, wife-swapping and dirty vicars, somehow span the entire spectrum of Sunday newspaper reading, and do so with enough original wit and sharpness of observation to neutralise such topics. A celebrated Python fancier and friend, particularly of Eric and Michael, the ex-Beatle George Harrison, says: "Let's face it. There are certain things in life which make life worth living, and one of those things is Python. Especially to someone like me. When you've gone through so much in life, and you're supposed to decide what is real and what isn't, you watch the television and you see all this madness going on, and everyone is being serious and accepting it, and you're ready to bang

your head on the wall in despair – then someone says 'And now for something completely different!' That saves the day. Laughter is the great release."

Philip Purser, writing in the *Sunday Telegraph* in January 1973, said: "What other popular entertainment in the world could have wrapped together in disrepute Edward VII, Wilde, Whistler, Shaw, Richard Attenborough, Pasolini, electrical goods, wife-swapping, the cloth and, oh yes, *Come Dancing*?"

The Pythons' second show at the Bavaria Atelier, Munich, unlike the first was made in English and later dubbed, much to the team's relief. It was later shown by the BBC as *Monty Pythons Fliegende Zirkus* with the subtitle *Schnapps with Everything* in October 1973. The Pythons also in that year embarked on a live stage tour

The only Monty Python's Flying Circus *show that followed a complete narrative was Mr Pither's Cycling Tour in the third series. Michael Palin played the unfortunate hero, making his way through the British Consulate in Smolensk which has gone Chinese, and awaiting a Russian firing squad.*

which took them to cities throughout Britain, on one-night stands. In spite of his diffidence at appearing in the television programmes, John Cleese enjoyed the experience of performing in front of live audiences. Their show was augmented by the appearance of Neil Innes, the talented musician-composer who had first come to the attention of Jones, Palin and Idle during the run of *Do Not Adjust Your Set,* when he had the Bonzo Dog Band.

After their United Kingdom tour the Pythons accepted an offer to go to Canada to repeat the experience. As they were crossing the Atlantic, and at a safe height of 31,000 feet, Cleese announced to the group that he would definitely not do any more television with the Pythons. Ahead lay a vastly more tiring tour than the British one, taking them from one side to the other of the second largest national land mass in the world. Their venues would range from small basement nightspots to vast auditoriums crammed with thousands of fans, their appetites whetted by the extensive showings the BBC programmes were now receiving on Canadian television.

On their return to England, after a short rest they played for a season at the Theatre Royal, Drury Lane, a large theatre normally associated with the most lavish Broadway musicals imported to London. But, while not averse to stage work, Cleese was adamant – no television. The group were in a dilemma since the BBC was now pressing for a fourth series. Eventually, it was decided that it would consist of only six shows as opposed to the previous thirteen, and that as some kind of subtle indication that the mix was not quite as before the words "Flying Circus" were dropped from the title.

"The group accepted my decision," said Cleese, "at least on the surface. And they went off and did their six shows, and they didn't apparently enjoy them that much. They didn't tell me immediately because it would have tended to confirm what I was already saying about doing

Terry Gilliam's graphics regularly enlivened the cover and pages of The Radio Times.

The Tudor job agency somehow becomes mixed up
with pornography smuggling. The sketch is terminated
by the arrival of a modern police inspector (Michael
Palin) who attempts to make a raid, but turns into Sir
Philip Sydney.

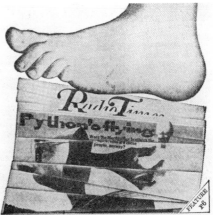

... and now for something entirely similar, Monty Python: 9.0 pm

more television. The shows were generally felt not to be as good as the first three series. I didn't actually think that. I didn't see all of them – I saw three, but I thought that two were every bit as good. But there seems to be a received opinion that they weren't as good."

The group had become unbalanced as well as jaded, with ideas proving harder to come by. Their success had been due to the formulation of a working method that enabled a group of strongly creative individuals to work coherently as a team. They did it without having a natural leader. But with Graham Chapman and John Cleese working together, as well as Michael Palin and Terry Jones, the Oxford–Cambridge balance prevailed, with Idle and Gilliam in the different camps. Thus the Cambridge contribution would be verbal, logical, literate, with absurdism arising often from the commonplace. The classic confrontation sketches usually emerged from the Cambridge side. Cleese's inspired, thesaurian gift for abuse would produce mounting crescendos of invective. The Palin-Jones imagination was much more visual and romantically inventive. Jones often directed film inserts and spent hours in the cutting room ensuring that the timing was right. "I was actually far more interested in form than John thinks," he says. "Particularly where *Holy Grail* was concerned. The Cambridge side said 'Let's put it in if it's funny'. Mike and I had to work very hard to make sure that lines went in that developed the plot, even if they weren't all that funny."

The most assertive team members, and each a leader of the respective factions, were Jones and Cleese. In frequent conflict, they nevertheless effectively countered one another. As the Python series progressed acrimony and squabbling in script meetings increased, leading to Cleese's disgusted comment: "Democracy gone mad!" But in spite of what some of the Pythons now look back on as spoiled, arrogant behaviour, the fusion of their respective energies usually produced a unified team product which for all its anarchy, unpredictability and insanity, flowed without a hint of inner conflict. In performance the Pythons worked with as-

John Cleese plays Dennis Moore, a famous 18th century highwayman, renowned for stealing lupins, in this elaborately dressed (and undressed) sketch in the show that opened the third Monty Python *series.*

Eating

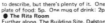

All restaurants reviewed provide food, except where stated. Prices quoted should not be taken as in any way indicative of prices actually charged, nor should the description of the restaurants be assumed to be in any way a description of the restaurants. Please let us know of any food you may have seen or been near recently.

● **The Vom-it**
7–9 North Circular, NW. 278 (a 7-hour walk)
Open 5 years a day.
Not licensed. Does not provide food of any sort, but Mr. & Mrs. Scrotum do their best to keep cheerful and encourage their customers to do the same. Help to while away the long hours by singing and talking about food. Plates are 2p and knives and forks 1p each.
● **Pukes**
Lower Bridge End Road Street, Barnet.

Open occasionally. 2.30 am'–6.00 pm. Not really worth a walk, but o.k. if you happened to be in Barnet and unable to get out. Some of the dishes include food, and one of our inspectors found a lump of marinated dough stuck to the underside of his plate. Worth examining the table-cloths and chair-seats, as either may well contain that extra portion.
● **Rita's Cafe**
25, The Building Site, Dalston.
Open 6–12. (279 9678). Closed.
A really good one. Probably the only really good one in London. Friendly. Cheery. Plenty of chat. Hardly any dead rats and good atmosphere. The tables may be a bit scruffy, but if you're a regular here, Rita herself will come and wipe them down with her own cloth. If you're new, don't be put off by the hostile glances, or the tendency to totally ignore you—it's well worth it for a glimpse of the food. Hard

to describe, but there's plenty of it. One plate of food: 5p. One mug of drink: 2p.
● **The Rita Room**
Further along, The Building Site, Dalston.
Open 6–12 (278 3456). Closed weekdays. This one used to belong to the Rita Chain, but has been bought up by Charles Forte. All the same features as Rita's, plus a full orchestra and expensively mounted floor-show. Stars have included: Tom Jones and Englebert Humperdinck and the staff of the Encyclopedia Britannica answering questions on gardening. Not a place to be seen by the in-crowd. Entertainment, plate of food and use of lavatory: £50 inc.

Flash One

● **Carmello's**
261 Cheyney Walk, SW.1
Open 10.00 pm.–2.00 pm. (last orders 10.30) (first orders 10.15 pm.)
Really fantastic! They have *food!* And what's more they give you this food if you pay them! Absolutely sensational! Soup is rather an expensive starter (20p) but it's hot and it really is great! And the main

courses are out of this world! They all include *meat!* Real meat! Meat in a kind of sauce (80p) was terrific! Meat on its own with potatoes done somehow (80p) was knockout! And the sweets are out of this world! Something in something else for 85p was unbelievable, and one of us had something else with something or other all over it for 90p which was just so far out I had to go to the toilet! Boy! Was that a good evening! Great! Just wait till I write it up! Hey! All those things on the wall! Too much! Those colours, man! Do you see those colours! And get that coffee! Oh boy! That coffee sure is something! It's *real* coffee! That is coffee! That is . . . coffee! The coffee is coffee-coloured! How about that? Look at it! Hey! It's in my cup and . . . (The rest of this review has been deleted and submitted as evidence—Ed.)

Film

'Aardvark' Hendon Classic. Till yesterday.

● **Hendon Classic**
'Aardvark': a rare and moving glimpse of a rare and moving animal. Till yesterday.
● **Gospel Oak Odeon**
'The Weather Forecast' (X) Graham Parker, Bert Foord. At last, the film of the successful BBC series. It's all there including the classic 'fog warning' and 'that's all from us till tomorrow, goodnight.' Some of the material has dated, but it's worth it for the superb rape scene.
● **Grays Inn Road Bioscope**
'Time Out at St. Trinian's': the film of the successful magazine. Mass self-abuse sequence shot at Harrow. Showing with 'Look at Life' No 48: Philip Jenkinson.
● **Playmate Cinema**
'Victor Lowndes Presents' (from midnight). The film of the millionaire (90 mins). The credit sequence is a little long (80 mins) but the rest of the film is nice and short.
● **Low Grade Cinema** (Ttnhm. Ct. Rd.)
'The Osmonds Live at the White House!': Watch the Nixons go wild! Tricia whipping herself into delirium, Pat positively writhing, even Richard is on his chair, cheering these great entertainers, by the end. Showing with 'Look at Life' No 176: Napalm.
● **Biograph**
The National Film Board of Canada presents **'Another Look at New Zealand'** (140 mins). Almost all of New Zealand is in this. + The New Zealand Film Board's award-winning **'Hello Canada'**: the slow-moving story of the Canadian countryside. It's been severely cut by its distributors from its original 3 hours to 7 minutes. Still too long.
● **ICA**
'Robert Having his Other Nipple Pierced' The sequel. This one features Mike Parkinson and introduces Nicholas Parsons to him. + **'4th Girl Required to Share'**: Not a film. A small ad. Go anyway. + **'Carry On Robert Having His Nipple Pierced'**: the usual crowd in the usual jokes.
● **Casino**
'McWhiter Bros.': How the West End was won. A moving story about a couple of brothers and their desperate struggle for publicity.
● **St. Martin's Hospital**
'Buckets of Blood Pouring out of People's Heads': (for times see local press). The new Peckinpah and none the more welcome for that. A loving and terribly honest look at some blood plasma.
● **Cineclub 24**
'Can I Have a Knighthood Please?': the new Richard Attenborough film. Richard directs this one with all the skill of a new-comer. An unusual story which suggest that the House of Windsor is directly descended from God. A moving portrayal of Elizabeth II (Flora Robson) ably supported by Warren Beatty as Charles; Ike and Tina Turner as Maggie and Tony; Richard Attenborough as Philip; and Anne wonderfully played by Anne Hayden-Jones and her husband Pip. Not a film to miss. A film to avoid at all costs. +
'Carry on Blood Island.'
● **Paradine Cinema**
'Hello, Good Evening and Welcome': the film of the frost. 'As moving as watching a shark at work' (Clive James).
● **Every Cinema**
'Carry on Bombing': the usual crowd in their latest romp, a light-hearted look at the White House. Nixon (Kenneth Williams) is anxious to win an election (Sid James) in time for Christmas (Hattie Jacques). His

team of bombers (Barbara Windsor, Charles Hawtrey, Joe Bugner) disguised as Santa Claus (Kenneth Connor) hilariously destroy large parts of South East Asia. 'A riot' (Evng. Nws.). + **'Ealing to Ongar'** (last train 1.05): the film of the Central Line. Quite good.

● **Cannon Row Police Station**
'It's the Fuzz' (from Tuesday). The zany whacky world of the PC seen through the eyes of the Drug Squad. Great rape scene. Some police pubes. Weak on bristols. + **'Carry on Nazi'**: the usual crowd camping it up in Nazi Germany. Worth it for Peter Butterworth's Goering.
● **Turnpike Lane Launderama**
'Up the Plaster' (N. Sherrin). British comedy at its most persistent. This is Ned's fifth film and it's really time he learned. Script by David Frost, Neil Shand, Pius XII, Rod Laver and Karl Mildenburger etc. from an original rewrite by Paul Fox Jr. + **'Carry on Developing'**: the usual crowd in the whacky story of some Merchant Bankers and their friends. Amusing-enough tale of the Finance House, Slater-Bombsite, and its attempt to fill the office blocks where London used to be. 'Recommended' (The Department of the Environment).
● **The Dirty Sinema**
'Come Again': Does it make you deaf? This Danish film won't help you find out as it's silent. Macs essential. No great rape scene, but then no Carry On either. + **'Death in Venice'** Stars Helmut Berger as a stinking transvestite who should have 'is face sawed off and the curvacious Charlotte Rampling as a piece of tail.' (Inspector Leopard, of the Yard.)
● **Tooting Classic**
'Carry On Blow Job': the usual crowd in a rather more unusual situation. Still good clean family viewing. A heart-breakingly dead one for the boys. + **'For Times See Local Press'**: great film. Continually recommended by Time Out.

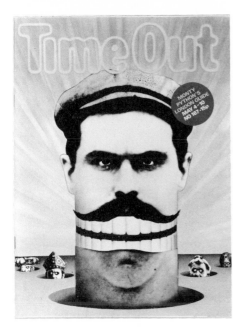

used to shoot forty minutes to cut it back to thirty, thereby discarding ten minutes, this time as part of a BBC economy drive they insisted that we only shot what we intended to use. It meant that we had no leeway there either. As it turned out, the best shows of that series were the third and the sixth."

The third show was indeed a classic, and included a sketch in which Eric Idle played a wartime squadron leader whose account of an encounter with the enemy is delivered in banter so arcane that his colleagues are completely mystified by it.

"Bally Jerry, pranged his kite right in the how's-your-father – hairy blighter, dicky-birded, feathered back on his sammy, took a waspy, flipped over on his Betty Harpers and caught his can in the Bertie."

A court-martial takes place in which Eric Idle, this time as a soldier, is accused of trivialising the war, flicking the enemy with wet towels and wearing special gaiters. Later Graham Chapman plays a man obsessed with the sounds of words, which he classifies as either "woody" or "tinny", while surrounded by a family reminiscent of a Shaftesbury Avenue drawing-room comedy of the Thirties. The programme ended with the only original serious song specially written for a Python show, *Where Does a Dream Begin?* by Neil Innes. The last show in the series, and the last of a total of forty-five broadcast by the BBC since October 1969, was transmitted on 5 December, 1974, and included the finals of The Worst Family in Britain, and an interview with Surrey housewife Mrs Ursula Hitler, who was puzzled in 1939 when she received an ultimatum on Poland from the then Prime Minister.

The Pythons wisely decided that they would move on. They had learned that it was essential for their artistic and financial wellbeing to control their own work in order not to be subjected to outside interference. Their albums (apart from the first which had been put out by BBC Enterprises) were produced by Charisma under contract, and had brought in substantial revenues for Python Productions, although it was not until the last one they made (called pointedly *Monty Python's Contractual Obligation Album*) that they

tonishing accord for each other, going far beyond mere acting, and whatever internal professional dissensions arose, they all held and hold each other in warm personal respect.

"Terry Jones is a very dominant personality," said Cleese, "and several of the group have said to me that when I was present Terry and I would lock horns, which kind of balanced us. But in the fourth series Terry dominated too much, and they felt that the balance of the group had gone. And also, my kind of input in the writing wasn't there. They used a bit of the material that Graham and I had written. But the balance of the group had changed. And after that *they* didn't want to do any more television, either."

"We were really at great disadvantages when we did the fourth series," said Terry Jones. "Not only had John gone, but whereas in the past we had always written the show well in advance, always giving us plenty of time for setting-up, rewriting, editing the film, recording the show, then choosing in which order they went out – we'd always have shot six of them before the series started, so that we could choose the funniest to begin with, but now we had no choice of order, as the series started almost immediately. And where before we

A script conference on the fourth series. Jones, Chapman and Palin with Neil Innes and director Ian MacNaughton.

got into the Top Twenty chart. They achieved it because the Independent Television Companies Association which vets broadcast advertising banned commercials for it on the grounds that the contents were offensive, thus providing the publicity for nothing, and then John Denver, whose publishers had given permission for a song to be used, took serious exception when he discovered that it was parodied in a version in which he was strangled. He sued for defamation, causing the track to be deleted.

In spite of the indifferent experience of film-making with Victor Lownes in 1971 the Pythons were intrigued with the idea of making films for theatrical release. The opportunity came in 1974 when with the assistance of the theatrical producer Michael White, who had put *Cambridge Circus* on in the West End, they formed a production company to make *Monty Python and the Holy Grail*. It was a low-

Above, *A poor couple who benefit from Dennis Moore's largesse – lupins*. Below, *John Cleese as the mayor feeling uneasy about the expertise of the sculptor (Graham Chapman) in the* Half a Bee *sketch.*

budget work, and White drummed up interest around the pop and rock world, getting Pink Floyd and Led Zeppelin to invest. The Pythons themselves worked for a mere £2,000 at the time, with a percentage of the gross returns.

"We'd all been convinced that we'd make a lot of money out of *And Now for Something Completely Different*," said Terry Jones, "but it came to about a thousand pounds, if it was anything at all. We still wanted to make a film and about the time of the third series we started writing a screenplay. We'd liked an idea of Mike's about King Arthur, and our first version was a mixture of old and new, with the Holy Grail being found in Harrod's. Harrod's, of course, had got everything! Then we took a year off from it. I'd got very heavily into the Middle Ages by then, and I thought it would be great to set it in one period so that we could give it an overall look."

John Cleese says that he always tells people that only ten per cent of the first

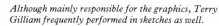
Although mainly responsible for the graphics, Terry Gilliam frequently performed in sketches as well.

who doesn't hiccough but tries to get things straight, a quite extraordinarily rude Frenchman and a three-headed knight. As the budget did not run to horses, mounted scenes were simulated to coconut shell accompaniment. An amazing duel was fought between Arthur and a Black Knight who carries on his gruesome contest until every one of his limbs is lopped off, and then threatens his retreating victor: "Come back here and take what's coming to you. I'll bite your legs off!" At the end of the film a modern police car bursts into view and an inspector, having arrested Arthur and his knights, puts his hand over the camera lens.

Both Terry Jones and Terry Gilliam directed, but all the Pythons were vocal in criticising the film's progress. "I usually agree with Terry G." said Terry Jones, "especially then. We had very similar ideas about things, a joint feeling. We talked about how we were going to divide it up. It got to be either certain scenes, or we alternated every other day. I enjoyed it but I think Terry found it a frustrating experience. The producer, Mark Forster, was always saying it's hopeless having two directors, you never know where you are, but I was a bit oblivious to it, I thought it worked well. But we had a loony schedule. On one occasion we produced ten minutes of cut film out of a single day's shooting."

With the release of *Monty Python and the Holy Grail* two things happened to the Pythons. The first was that each went away to separate enterprises of their own, and in some cases brought to fruition projects that they had been contemplating for a considerable time before, but had never had the time to pursue. The second was that they began to make real money at last. "We had made a good living by BBC standards after being together for six years," said John Cleese. "I used to get £240 per show, and probably £150 for writing it – so for seven months' work I would make something like five or six thousand. Well, on that sort of money you don't think you're going to go to the West Indies for three weeks. *Grail* was put together the

draft screenplay survived into the final draft. Although eschewing further Python television, he was delighted to be part of the film.

Monty Python and the Holy Grail is an extraordinary movie. The Pythons published a remarkably comprehensive book on its making which includes early draft scripts, notes, the production script, stills, Gilliam drawings, and a complete, full audited statement of the production costs right down to the amounts spent on wigs and props. It totalled £229,575, which in the light of its subsequent box-office performance, was exceptionally modest. The device of medieval characters talking and acting in the manner of people today was mixed up with scenes of an almost poetic beauty, shot in remote Scottish locations to the discomfort of all involved. The story was fragmented into a series of absurd encounters with such characters as the Knights who Say "Ni!", the guard

way we put the television shows together. And then in 1975 we started getting our royalties on it."

Cleese, in association with Connie Booth from whom he had separated and would soon be divorced, wrote and starred in *Fawlty Towers*, their legendary situation comedy series for the BBC. The parting of the spouses had become inevitable, but they remained on good enough terms to have a happy working relationship.

Basil Fawlty, hotelier, the owner of a small residential establishment in the leafy coastal resort of Torquay, was boorish, insensitive, quick-tempered, impatient, hen-pecked and cowardly, a bully whose manner could switch from oily obsequiousness to hair-tearing hysteria in a flash. Cleese, having based the character on a genuine prototype he had come across on a Devon film location in the early days of Python, had already used the character in a script for the *Doctor* series produced by Humphrey Barclay. John and Connie were anxious to write together, and within an hour of sitting down realised that a hotel offered a perfect venue for a comedy show, since there was no need to justify the introduction of new characters, however eccentric – all they had to do was just walk in as guests.

Part of the success of the programme was due to the selection and delineation of the stock characters. Leading the cast were Prunella Scales as Basil's imperturbable wife, Sybil, who remained maddeningly sane during his manic outbursts, Connie as Polly, a charming, but put-upon maid-of-all-work, an art student filling in time with some work experience, and Manuel, a Spanish waiter with next to no command of English and the constant butt of Fawlty's verbal and physical bullying, played devastatingly well by Andrew Sachs.

Fawlty Towers went out in two series, the first in 1975, the second in 1979, each of six episodes. The ranting rudeness and sarcasm of Fawlty, and his ability to turn a minor setback into a major catastrophe, made for one of the greatest comic monsters ever seen on television, but the comedy went far beyond superficial farce, and on occasion viewers were disturbed by his crassness, so believably had his vic-

John Cleese framed by the TV screen finally bowed out from the fourth series.

tims been drawn. When the BBC entered one of the episodes in the Montreux Festival, one in which Fawlty has the problem of a dead guest on his hands while entertaining a party of Germans, it was not well received. It had not helped that it played at nine a.m. on the Sunday morning, with the sound not working. A huffy Swiss observed that only the English find foreigners funny, and foreigners included the Swiss. Yet in spite of all that *Fawlty Towers* was a record-breaking export for the BBC, but Cleese resisted the tempting offers to milk the idea for a further series, or a feature film, although books of the scripts were published.

He had also started, in association with Anthony Jay, a television writer with a pedagogic inclination, Video Arts, a company that produced training films for commerce and industry – their intention

being to impart lessons on the operation of business methods with Cleesian wit. Jay had been the writer of the main theme back in the days of *The Frost Report* and was always a great believer in the use of television for purposes other than mere entertainment. Video Arts was not expected to make vast returns, but in recent years has become so profitable that Cleese is obliged to keep it going rather than sell it off and face the tax blow. Such has been its success that it even won the Queen's Award for Exports in 1982. Of all the Pythons, Cleese remains the best-known and possibly the most successful in financial terms. He is able to command high fees from advertising, particularly from Sony for whom he was under contract to make commercials promoting their audio and video equipment. ("The conceited, slit-eyed little buggers!")

Eric Idle also struck out on his own, creating his television comedy series, called *Rutland Weekend Television*. There were two series of *RWT* and a Christmas special, and it led to one of Idle's most brilliant inventions – the Rutles.

The origin of the Rutles came from a mock-pop group in one of the *RWT* shows called the Rutland Stones, and Neil Innes had written a Beatles parody for them. On a visit to America hosting the NBC comedy show *Saturday Night Live* Idle showed a clip of the song, billing the group as the Rutles. *All You Need is Cash* followed, a bogus documentary of the lives of four Liverpudlian musicians who bear extraordinary resemblance to their real-life counterparts. To add to the joke, one of the Beatles, George Harrison, appears in the film as a music journalist. Footage of real Beatles' incidents was spliced in and matched, while Neil Innes composed several songs neatly in their style. There was an enormous effort made to get the atmosphere right, and even the films the Beatles made for Dick Lester and the cartoon *The Yellow Submarine* were parodied. In many respects it was too painfully close to the real thing, and

Monty Python And The Holy Grail, *the first Python-produced feature film, was shot on a low budget in Scotland. Horses were out, knights had to walk.*

loaded with so many references that would only make sense to dedicated Beatles-followers its in-jokes incomprehensible to an audience unfamiliar with the career of the Fab Four. The subsequent recording had mock album covers for its album cover – with sleeve artwork for *Meet the Rutles, Sgt Rutter's Darts Club Band, Tragical History Tour* and *Let it Rot* faithfully reproduced.

Terry Gilliam, anxious to move away from animation, turned to film-making. In collaboration with Charles Alverson, he fashioned a screenplay called *Jabberwocky*, vaguely based on Lewis Carroll's poem, and it was reproduced as a film by Sandy Lieberson and John Goldstone. Although Michael Palin played the lead – the young cooper's apprentice who is taken for a prince and finds himself expected to destroy a terrifying dragonlike creature that is wreaking havoc throughout the nation – and Terry Jones appeared as a poacher, it was not a Python film, but a personal project. Sharing with Terry Jones and Michael Palin a fascination for the Middle Ages, he created an astonishingly detailed view of life in his imaginary kingdom. The almost masochistic wallowings in mud and worse in uncomfortable costumes that characterised so much of the location-filmed inserts in the Python shows reached a mucky apotheosis in *Jabberwocky*. Tons of garbage were strewn over the street set at Shepperton Studios which had originally been constructed for the film musical *Oliver*, and the actors were required to make their way through it without allowing their nostrils to betray distaste. Even the king, Bruno the Questionable, a crumbling baroque performance by a toothless Max Wall, is required to pick pieces of the the palace ceiling out of his meals. A bizarre jousting scene in which unseen knights are brutally dispatched, the camera staying on the royal box as the king and his entourage are drenched with torrential downpours of blood, caused tremors of disgust when a double-page spread of the scene was published in colour by *The Sunday Times*. The climax of this comedy of horrors was reached with the appearance of the Jabberwock itself, a monstrous sauropod more disgusting of aspect than anything drawn by Hieronymous Bosch or Gerald Scarfe. Gilliam's appetite for the grotesque extended itself all over the film, which divided the critics, some of whom were unable to take the ceaseless onslaught of scatology, the dung and defecation jokes, or the severed limbs and gore. But Roy Smith's production design and Terry Bedford's camera work impressively abetted the director's quest for a vivid medieval atmosphere, so powerful that one could almost smell it.

Graham Chapman also turned to films, co-producing, writing and starring in *The Odd Job*, which was directed by Peter Medak. It was based on a television play by Bernard McKenna and was about a man who is such a failure that he cannot even handle his own suicide, but has to hire an odd-job man (played by David Jason) to do it for him. With a change of circumstances the need for extreme action passes, but he is unable to cancel the order, and the film is a black comedy in which a number of uninvolved people get killed as various attempts to fulfil the contract are bungled. The film secured neither good notices nor much of a release. From the outset the project had suffered – the odd-job man was originally going to be played by the gifted, crazy rock star Keith Moon of The Who, but when the time came for shooting he was incapacitated through chronic drinking, and in hospital. A year later he was dead from an overdose of drugs mixed with alcohol. Medak was not the first choice of director, either – originally Cliff Owen was to have made it, but he broke a thigh and had to be replaced at short notice. Chapman continued, in spite of the failure, to collaborate with McKenna, and with Peter Cook on the script for the pirate film which was eventually to become *Yellowbeard*.

Michael Palin, apart from acting in a BBC film of Jerome K. Jerome's *Three Men in a Boat*, which was directed by Stephen Frears, and playing the principal role in Gilliam's *Jabberwocky*, collaborated with Terry Jones on the television comedy series, *Ripping Yarns*. The pilot, produced and directed by Terry Hughes

Eric Idle and Graham Chapman in Monty Python And The Holy Grail.

who had suggested the project to the duo, was *Tomkinson's Schooldays*, in which every convention of school life was sent up, from the school bully keeping Filipino women in his rooms to the crucifixion of junior offenders against the code on the stone walls. The BBC consented to a total of nine films before calling a halt.

Terry Jones turned to Chaucer. "Since about 1970 I had been beavering away on Chaucer in my spare time, and suddenly I found I could take a year off to write my book. I've always felt that Chaucer was a good guy. What infuriates the academics is that I have studied him from the historical viewpoint, whereas they look at him purely as literature, and thus miss an enormous amount of what he is saying. When I've given talks at universities I've sensed their hostility." His resulting work, *Chaucer's Knight*, amounts to convincing proof that this prominent character in *The Canterbury Tales* was scarcely

Filming The Holy Grail *was arduous, mainly on account of itchy costumes, heavy rain and two directors.*

a "verray, parfit, gentil knyght" but a bloodthirsty mercenary roaming the eastern Mediterranean butchering for booty. His book is far from the dabbling of a comedian in a peripheral area as a dilettante, but an impressive work of scholarship composed in a lucid, readable style and the product of a fresh and imaginative approach to a subject that has suffered from decades of hackneyed, sterile teaching in British schools. That the return for his investment of time and research materials made the whole venture wildly uneconomic served to enhance its validity, but the academic critics tended to disapprove of the poaching on their turf.

Thus all the Pythons found absorbing pursuits of their own outside the group. Yet *Monty Python* had become institutionalised into a cult, particularly in the United States. Their first appearance on American television had been dire, coming at the end of their Canadian tour. They had guested on the Johnny Carson show *Tonight* for NBC, with Joey Bishop as the host. Their appearance was re-

The team take a break to reflect upon the potential financial success of their efforts.

ceived by an uncomprehending audience, who could not understand what was so funny about a bunch of Britishers wearing drag and screeching at each other in hysterical feminine voices. However, the Public Broadcasting Service, which bought a great deal of BBC output, started running *Monty Python* shows, the first being transmitted by KERA, the PBS station in Dallas, where the manager, Ron Devillier, had become a convert. In spite of apprehensions that the show was too parochial, especially in its constant references to the BBC style of television presentation, which is somewhat different from that in the United States, it quickly built up a following, particularly among young campus viewers. Students visiting Britain had soon heard of the Pythons, and took their albums and books back with them, acquiring the taste. PBS stations all over America found *Monty Python* was one of their most popular pro-

DO NOT DELAY
WNET/13
NEWSFILM
DO NOT DELAY
WNET/13
NEWSFILM
DO NOT DELA
WNET/13
NEWSFILM
13
WNET

grammes, and its success was boosted in 1975 with the release of *Monty Python and the Holy Grail*, each feeding off the other's triumph. It was even found that commercial stations were taking the show on a local basis in some areas. A promotional tour by the Pythons to promote *Holy Grail* kindled yet more interest, and one of the three major networks, ABC, decided to climb on the *Circus* bandwagon. They had a show filling a ninety-minute slot called *Wide World of Entertainment*, and decided to bid for the whole of the fourth Python series – which consisted of six half-hour shows – with the intention of running them in two groups of three. The BBC failed initially to appreciate that in a ninety-minute timeslot there will be twenty-four minutes of commercials, making it impossible on that basis to transmit the programmes exactly as they had been seen on British television. When realisation finally dawned it was too late. On 3 October at the late hour of 11.30 pm ABC broadcast their first show. The Pythons themselves had to wait until the following month when Nancy Lewis, who runs their American interests, came to

The Pythons take part in a telethon for Channel 13 in New York, the PBS station. It was KERA the PBS station in Dallas which initially carried their Python shows.

London with a videotape. They watched it with horror. Not only had the cuts for commercials been made in a crude, arbitrary manner, but the programmes themselves had been re-edited, key phrases had been excised, jokes toned down so that they were no longer funny, and the dead hand of censorship heavily applied. They learned that the second ABC compilation was due for transmission on the day after Christmas, and they tried to get the BBC to intervene. They also asked ABC to give them an opportunity to do the edit themselves, but the network refused. The Pythons then decided to apply for an injunction in New York to delay the broadcast. They wanted a full hearing of their case, which was that the show was going out bearing their names, yet did not meet with their approval, and was damaging to their reputation.

Terry Gilliam, being an American citizen, and accompanied by Michael Palin, flew to New York to plead for them. ABC offered to show them both the tape of the show, which they viewed and found completely unacceptable. There was no hope for an out of court settlement, and the respective parties next faced each other in a courtroom, flanked by expensive attornies. The lawyer for ABC made an unsuccessful attempt to allege that the Pythons were bringing the action in order to publicise their live stage appearance in New

York three weeks hence, but had failed to do his research properly. They were not due for another four months (although their show was going to *run* for three weeks). A full account of what followed is contained in Chapter IV of Robert Hewison's thorough, excellently documented and fair book, *Monty Python: The Case Against*. It was an important case, not just for the Pythons but for all who wrote and performed their work for television. The network argued that their right to edit should be absolute as they had the responsibility for protecting the hundreds of stations that ran their output. The paradox of American television is that the commercial networks, while putting out

matter often of stultifying banality, exercise a far more rigid code of censorship than PBS; in other words, they act with what they consider far greater responsibility than the so-called public service.

The judge accepted most of the Pythons' arguments (they had behaved themselves with great decorum in spite of the occasional lunacies of the proceedings which could almost have formed part of a Monty Python sketch), but ruled that an injunction preventing transmission at such short notice would cause an unreasonable financial loss to ABC. However, he ordered that the show would have to carry a disclaimer that it had been edited without the Pythons' approval and that

The Pythons become a cult success in the United States after many television and live appearances. Their apogee was their series of performances at the Hollywood Bowl in front of an audience of 8,000 each night which was recorded on film. Above, Eric Idle and Michael Palin as disrobed judges. Above right, the Lumberjack Song.

they wished to dissociate themselves from it. ABC then went to the Appeal Court and won a stay of execution, and the show was duly broadcast with the words 'Edited for television by ABC', which could mean almost anything and certainly weren't sufficient to indicate the Pythons' disapproval.

It was not, however, the end of the matter. The Pythons appealed against the denial of an injunction, and after several months succeeded in preventing ABC from ever screening their shows again, and also establishing that the copyright in their scripts was their own, and that a network had no licence to re-edit or amend their material at will. In that respect the Pythons established an important precedent in copyright law in the United States, and strengthened the rights of the writer in determining how his material should be used. They also gained the copyright in their programmes outside the United Kingdom in lieu of damages, and the BBC was obliged to deliver tapes of all forty-five shows, along with the two ABC compilations. With the rise in the late seventies and early eighties of domestic video it can only be a matter of time before the shows will be re-released on pre-recorded videotapes, and the team have the comforting thought that they are sitting on a healthy, unrealised asset.

Having enjoyed the experience of working apart the Pythons decided that another film together might not be such a bad idea. *Holy Grail* profits had been substantial, especially in view of the low initial budget, and when the team came together in 1976 for the Amnesty one-night benefit, *Pleasure at Her Majesty's* (without Eric) it amounted to a major reunion of the Oxbridge wits (Alan Bennett, John Bird, Eleanor Bron, John Fortune, Jonathan Miller, Peter Cook, Dudley Moore, Tim Brooke-Taylor, Graeme Garden and Bill Oddie were also in the cast) and a joyous euphoria prevailed. The mood was set fair for the team's three-week appearance at the City Center, New York, and enthusiasm for a new film increased. Eric Idle had, during a promotional tour for *Holy Grail*, quipped to a reporter when asked what the next Python film might be: *"Jesus Christ - Lust for Glory!"* When discussions began in earnest to seek a theme, they kept returning to a biblical motif. It was, they felt, an area ripe for sending up. Not only was the ground stony with taboos and problems of taste, but as a genre of cinema it was noted for the turgid, overblown spectacles of Cecil B. DeMille. They began thinking on the lines of an alternative life of Christ,

and then switched to a new character who just happened to be present during the important moments of his life, a sort of thirteenth apostle who kept arriving too late to make any impact on history.

The script gestation period turned out to be long as ideas were adopted and discarded. The Python method by which each individual's work is scrutinised and criticised collectively meant that more than a year passed before a first draft was finally put together, in which time the idea of *Brian of Nazareth*, the man who just happened to be around during the lifetime of Jesus, had taken some sort of shape. They decided that the next stage in which the draft would be tuned into a filmable script should be a winter working holiday, away from wives, girlfriends, children, agents and other distractions, and Eric, the traveller, nominated Barbados as a suitable venue. Barry Spikings, then in

A motley crew of artistes come together for the 1976 Amnesty Show at Her Majesty's Theatre. Back row, left to right, *Alan Bennett, John Cleese, Jonathan Lynn, Michael Palin, Bill Oddie, Graham Chapman, John Fortune, Jonathan Miller, Desmond Jones, Graeme Garden.* Front: *Carol Cleveland, Terry Jones, Neil Innes, Peter Cook, Eleanor Bron and John Bird.*

charge of the film side of EMI, also happened to be taking a sojourn in the sun, and was intrigued by the Pythons' presence. As they had embarked on the *Brian* project speculatively, hoping that they would secure a production deal on the strength of a finished screenplay, Spikings decided to involve EMI. On his return to London he immediately contacted the Pythons' producer, John Goldstone, and after deliberations, secured an agreement for EMI to back the film with a budget of $4.5 million, a sum which compared handsomely with the paltry amount on which *Monty Python and the Holy Grail* was made, and took them into an entirely different league.

It meant that foreign locations were possible, and as Tunisia had been used for the ambitious television mini-series *Jesus of Nazareth*, directed by Franco Zeffirelli, and several sets had been left standing *in*

situ, the two Terrys flew off to do some scouting, while production and costume designs were turned into reality, and shooting was scheduled to commence in April 1978.

At this point, the influence of the aforementioned Mrs Whitehouse, self-appointed guardian of national morals, was suddenly felt. She had, by great zeal and determination, brought her private prosecution against the newspaper *Gay News*, and its editor Denis Lemon, for giving space to what she considered was a blasphemous poem in that it suggested a

homosexual attraction between a Roman centurion and Christ on the cross. The prosecution, the first for blasphemous libel since the Twenties, succeeded, and the unfortunate Lemon was fined and given a suspended prison sentencě. The Whitehousian wrath had been directed not merely at blasphemers, but at homosexuals, who were normally beyond her reach. Understandably, Graham Chapman was very concerned about the case, having financed the launch of *Gay News* and as an active supporter of the rights of homosexuals. In February 1978 the appeal was heard and dismissed, although the suspended sentence was quashed.

Meanwhile, the Pythons were allowing pre-production costs to mount up, confident of EMI's backing. They also understood that they would have sole artistic control. Then came a bombshell. Barry Spikings was told by his chief executive, Lord Delfont, that it would be impossible for EMI to finance the film as it stood, that the Pythons' demand for control was not desirable and that the costs were getting out of hand. Clearly, it was the possibility of blasphemy that perturbed Delfont, a Jew but possessing what he regarded as a sacred obligation to the Christian patrons of EMI theatres. It was Delfont's personal decision, but Spikings was left with the uncomfortable task of informing Goldstone that the film was off.

The Pythons were now sorely out of pocket. EMI eventually paid over a small proportion of the expenses, but for a while it looked as though the project was doomed. Talks with other film companies got nowhere. Help came, however, from an unlikely source. George Harrison, the ex-Beatle, had as his business partner Denis O'Brien, a formidable figure in the world of finance and a merchant banker who had worked with Rothschild's. "When I heard about the Python film, because they were friends of mine (especially Eric and Michael) and because I wanted to see their movie I had a word with Denis – 'How can we help my mates?' And a little while later Denis rang me back and said 'OK, I've figured a way to get it made,' and he got it rolling." It was the beginning of HandMade Films, now an important force in British film produc-

The Pythons performed in Amnesty International Benefits. Left, Cleese and Jones, in Pleasure At Her Majesty's *1976,* top, *assisted by newscasterette Anna Ford. Above, Pamela Stephenson and John Cleese in* The Secret Policeman's Other Ball, *1981. Graham Chapman as the policeman is also about to strip.*

tion, a company with an interesting track record thanks to Harrison's enthusiasm, O'Brien's acumen, and a sound professional team.

Production got underway six months later than was intended. Direction was this time solely in the hands of Terry Jones, with Terry Gilliam as the production designer. As usual, all the Pythons were vociferous in their contributions and played several roles apiece, although that of the eponymous Brian fell upon Graham Chapman. The title was finally confirmed as *Monty Python's Life of Brian*, and the finished film went through several edits before being considered ready for the critics. It is another Pythonic principle that their material is ruthlessly pre-tested, first among themselves, and then, where their films are concerned, with preview audiences.

It was clear that they had gone to some trouble to ensure that no-one who saw the film could possibly confuse their Judean hero for Christ. At the beginning the three wise men burst into the stable where a shrewish woman (inevitably Terry Jones) is giving birth. She harangues them in spite of their gifts, and it is only when they spot that down the road there's *another* stable bright with light do they realise that they have got the wrong manger. Later there's a Sermon on the Mount scene in which Christ speaks too indistinctly for those on the fringe of the crowd to appreciate what he's saying. At the end of the film there is a crucifixion scene, but it is not just Brian who is hanging from a cross, but dozens of other miscreants, who join Eric Idle in singing his jaunty, cheerful, optimistic song about looking on the bright side which is then heard over the end titles. In fact, as any historian can confirm, crucifixion was a common Roman punishment and such mass executions did occur.

The humour in the film to a large extent depends on the juxtaposition of historical settings and characters with modern attitudes and modes of speech. The People's Liberation Front of Judea, a terrorist organisation plotting to kidnap Pilate's wife and other heinous acts to demoralise the occupiers of their country, conduct their clandestine meetings like the convening of a bunch of trade union shop stewards. "What have the Romans ever done for us?" says Cleese as their leader, and then grudgingly, but with a scrupulous regard for fair play, compiles a list of social improvements that their invaders have brought about, so that the committee's statement cannot be faulted for inaccuracy. The film shows a people desperately looking for a Messiah, so much so that for

a time they believe that Brian is indeed the one.

The *Gay News* case had altered the climate in which the film was to open. Although the majority of people in Britain were not likely to object, the legal finding of blasphemy had sharpened the axes of the Festival of Light, who without having seen the film, denounced it. The British Board of Film Censors, a voluntary body appointed by the industry to issue a certificate to all films shown in British cinemas, had been formed generations earlier to protect the industry from many scores of local authority bodies throughout the country who felt a right to vet everything that would play in their areas. In this instance, the BBFC was unwilling to issue any rating until legal opinions had been sought. In Canada a radio programme about the making of the film was banned by CBC, who had already dropped the Python television series, and faced a demonstration of McGill students in Montreal dressed as Gumbies (was it "The Lumberjack Song", with its Mounties outraged by a transvestite woodcutter that had offended the state-run broadcasting system?). Their action gave Methuen, the Pythons' publishers, great qualms, and the elaborate book of the film that they were preparing was in jeopardy. But in August 1979 the BBFC passed the film without cuts, awarding it an AA certificate, which meant that it was restricted to the over-fourteens. In the United States the film opened the same month with an R rating, indicating that it could be shown to those under seventeen if accompanied by an adult. However, attacks were immediately mounted by religious organisations of several faiths, with Catholics condemning it, thus making it a sin to go to a showing. A pressure group, Citizens Against Blasphemy, was formed and attempted without success to bring a prosecution. However, demonstrations and denunciations flourished, and clearly most of the protesters were basing their outrage on what they supposed was in the film. William Buckley, the articulate right-wing *New York Post* columnist, even thought that Monty Python himself was crucified at the end of the film, a conclusion that had never occurred to the

makers. When it went on release in America the great Bible Belt became incensed and in many small towns in southern and south-western states local pressures caused it to be banned or terminated in mid-run. Nevertheless, the publicity engendered by the controversy helped to ensure a healthy box-office return in the places where it was allowed to be seen without interference, and the film was already in profit by the time it opened in London in November.

The Festival of Light, aware that the fuss in America had been unhelpful to their cause, changed their tactics and adopted a more low-key approach, lobbying local authorities to overrule the BBFC and ban the film outright in their areas. In spite of the presence of the

Python movies led to best-selling books and record albums, although the group has resisted attempts to turn them into an international marketing corporation.

BBFC such local options are possible but rarely carried out, except in certain areas notorious for their refusal to conform with the classifications. When *The Life of Brian* opened, John Cleese and Michael Palin appeared on a BBC chat show hosted by Tim Rice, and were savagely attacked by the Bishop of Southwark and Malcolm Muggeridge, who had seen the film earlier in the day. A fierce one-sided argument developed, the Bishop suggesting that they would get their thirty pieces of silver for it. Cleese's protestation that the film was really about closed minds not being prepared to question faith rather than an attack on faith itself, was glossed over by their voluble critics. It was Tim Rice's first experience of hosting a chat show. "I just left them to get on with it," he says.

The film was banned outright in some parts of Britain, including Surrey, Hereford, much of Berkshire, Cornwall, West Yorkshire, and in other places it was uprated to an X-certificate which kept the under-eighteens away entirely. One district council took pleasure in banning it, even though there were no cinemas within its purlieu.

In spite of such notoriety, and to some extent because of it, the film was a financial success and the thirty pieces of silver did accrue. The Pythons moved on to other things of their own. Graham Chapman published his autobiography which veered from straight fact to absurdist nonsense, and was titled *A Liar's Autobiography Volume VI*. Terry Gilliam published *Animations of Mortality*, a book on his graphic methods, using illustrations from many of the *Monty Python* animated sequences. Terry Jones finally saw *Chaucer's Knight* into print, and also wrote a collection of children's fairy tales, which were published in an edition illustrated by Michael Foreman. John Cleese played Petruchio in Jonathan Miller's BBC television production of *The Taming of the Shrew*, a move into a new area for him, which met with critical approval. Eric Idle, having written his novel, *Hello Sailor*, then wrote a play *Pass the Butler* which had a disappointingly short West End run. Michael Palin worked on a screenplay with Gilliam for the film *Time Bandits*, premiered in 1981.

The financial backing for *Time Bandits* again came from HandMade Films. With an idea behind it that was perverse and original, it was of particular appeal to children. The bandits of the title were a band of marauding dwarfs who have stolen a map of the universe and are thus able to roam at will through any era they care to choose, taking with them a young boy from his suburban bedroom to meet Agamemnon and Robin Hood and a

'Always look on the bright side of life ...'

172

Terry Jones/Mandy, directing The Life of Brian.

somewhat disappointing Napoleon. The first hint of anything unusual occurs after young Kevin has gone to bed and a knight in armour suddenly leaps out of his bedroom wall. The dwarfs are a rambunctious, competitive assortment, constantly jockeying for power and each imbued with unique idiosyncrasies. Robert Hewison likens them to the Pythons themselves. John Cleese appears briefly in the film as Robin Hood, acting the part rather as if he's modelled on the Duke of Kent, and Agamemnon is played by Sean Connery. The climax of the film, an extended battle between good and evil as personified by Ralph Richardson and David Warner, takes place in a huge celestial fortress, and there are many echoes of that great work, *The Wizard of Oz*. As fantasy it has a hard edge, something that has more appeal to children than squeamish adults. It did moderate business in Britain, but in the United States it became an important box-office contender, and reaped satisfying rewards for its makers. It is another personal film for Terry Gilliam, and contains within it the promise of a rich cinematic imagination that will undoubtedly yield more treasures in due course. His next project, the collaboration with the playwright Tom Stoppard, tentatively entitled *Brazil*, was in hand in the summer of 1983.

Michael Palin did not direct the next film he wrote, although it, too, was very much his creation, and was also financed by HandMade. *The Missionary* is the story of a returned exile from Africa. Exposed is the double standard of Edwardian life, the hypocrisies of class and manners, and the grotesque undersurface of the period, tacitly accepted by the ruling class. It is an extremely beautiful film to look at, and director Richard Loncraine invested the compositions with soft, misty colours like genre painters of the day, and demonstrated the principle that Michael Palin has so long endorsed, that comedy is better if it looks good as well. There are perhaps too many themes in the film, a surfeit of plot ideas which tend to cancel each other out. But it is convincing evidence that Michael Palin's talents are somewhat special

In 1980 the Pythons performed live at the Hollywood Bowl for four nights before an audience of 8,000, which was deliberately limited to half the normal capacity. Even so, the crowd was vast and huge video screens were set up on each side of the podium. The fans greeted each well-known number, be it the Parrot Sketch or The Lumberjack Song or the Custard Pie Lecture, as though they were the Golden Hits of Frank Sinatra, and those present were aware of a mellowing, relaxed style of confident men. John Cleese wandered among the seated throng hawking "Albatross – fresh albatross!" and Graham Chapman reprised his celebrated one-man wrestling act. Among happy outcomes of the brief appearance in Los Angeles was the meeting between John and his second wife, Barbara Trentham, who was quoted as saying: "It was mild curiosity at first sight."

Again the Pythons, enjoying their occasional get-togethers, felt the urge to make another film. The emergent product was *Monty Python's The Meaning of Life*, an all-embracing title that had something in common with the unbeatable comprehensiveness of *Flash Gordon Conquers the Universe*. The usual months of fretting over themes and scripts went on, but a decision was taken to drop any attempt at a straightforward continuous narrative, and instead to construct it from a series of largely self-contained sketches, each illuminating the seven ages of man from birth until the visitation of the Grim Reaper, with a glimpse of the hereafter. The final draft was hammered out in a sun-drenched island of the West Indies, again, in this case Jamaica, and it was decided that Terry Jones would be the director, with Terry Gilliam in charge of something called The Other Unit, which would prepare footage to run alongside the main picture. Much to Denis O'Brien's disappointment the team accepted a deal from a Hollywood major, Universal, who were prepared not to interfere with the script,

a concession that the Python producer John Goldstone successfully negotiated. Denis O'Brien had scared the group with his ambitious financial plans, and while he sincerely believed that with successful marketing he could have made each of them into multi-millionaires, they remained uninterested.

"The Pythons don't like being leant on," says Michael Palin. "The more we're leaned on, the more we bridle. The BBC tried it. ABC wanted to make us stars on the network. We sued to have it taken off. Whenever heavy commercial pressures are put on the Pythons we always react against it. Denis, with the best will in the world, tried to line us up with big corporations in America to sell our material – we were offered shares in companies and that kind of thing – and for a month it all seemed wonderful. Then we all looked at each other and said 'This is not our world – we're not really happy here.' End of Python International Corporation. Back to our little office in Cambridge Gate and all the people we've worked with before."

The Meaning of Life starts from man's evolution from fish, and at the beginning the group is seen as the residents of a large tank. "The fish costumes were dreadful," said John, who traditionally has always complained most about the discomforts inflicted by some Python members on the rest. For him the film was a tedious experience. Terry Jones, as ever representing the contrary position, thought that it went like a dream.

Adopting the procedure they followed after *The Life of Brian*, the film was shown to small groups in rough-cut form around Christmas 1982. As a consequence of those screenings several changes were made, the most drastic of which was the removal of the Terry Gilliam pirate sequence from the central part of the picture, and making it into a separate, preceding featurette. Initially, Terry Gilliam had been reluctant to return to animation, but given a budget in excess of his wildest dreams, he found the challenge irresistible, and produced some of his finest work. He also designed the title sequence for the main film, clearly establishing it in the mainstream of the Python tradition.

In *The Meaning of Life* there is something to offend everyone. The manifold targets include the medical profession, birth control, sex education, consumerism, greed, religion, American tourists and just about everything else. One justly acclaimed sequence has Michael Palin as a gritty northerner, newly redundant, coming home to face a multitude of children that have resulted from his eschewal of contraception as a good Catholic. Having announced that they will have to be sold for medical experimentation, a wild and ambitiously staged production number takes place involving an enormous corps de ballet of unemployed workers, urchins, housewives, cardinals, nuns, high-kicking to a Palin ditty "Every Sperm is Sacred!" In another section of the film John Cleese plays a master in a public school teaching his bored class practical sex, using his wife as a visual aid. The boys act with as much hostile indifference as if the subject had been irregular Latin verbs.

The most revolting sketch of all has Terry Jones as Mr Creosote, the richest, fattest man in the world, dining in an expensive restaurant, and vomiting copiously, having demanded the menu and a bucket from the snobbish, unctous head waiter, performed by John Cleese. Eventually, the disgusting diner explodes and showers the entire establishment with cascades of vomit. The vegetable soup used to simulate it began to acquire un-

Above left, *The* Daily Mirror *was scarce on the Tunisian location, hence John Cleese's anxiety.* Below left, *Terry Gilliam and Eric Idle enjoy a joke.* Top, *Graham Chapman as Brian with Terry Jones as his mother, the dreadful Mandy.* Centre and below, *The mob pursues Brian believing him to be The Messiah. Brian manages to get a few paces in front of the mob but is nevertheless unable to avoid eventual capture.*

pleasant olfactory qualities after three days' filming, and Cleese was not the only Python to find the scene uncomfortable to perform as well as to watch.

The film opened in London in June 1983 after a successful run in the United States. At the Cannes Film Festival it was a British competition entry and to the astonishment of the Pythons, and to certain of the critics, it was awarded the Special Jury Prize, the second highest honour available.

Whither Python? After *The Meaning of Life* the question that was constantly asked was whether it was their swansong or would they in the fullness of time come together again. Opinions differed, even among themselves, depending on the mood of the day. One Python would say that he could never envisage them not

doing something together in the future, but another would aver vehemently that he never wanted to work with them again – lunch, yes, dinner, yes, but work, forget it! Anne James, who manages the Python office in Cambridge Gate, with its western outlook across the leafy acreage of Regents Park, and who has been with them since *Holy Grail* days, says: "What any of them say this month will be different next month – you can be sure of that. Once they're all together in this room it's amazing how things take shape. They may all be different people, but they have a tremendous group loyalty. We shall see!"

The man who brought them all together in the first place, Barry Took, on the other hand, thinks that it is all over. "They're in the forties now, and they're all doing other things. Why should they work themselves silly over a six-way split? They don't have to do it."

Three of the six Pythons became involved in *Yellowbeard*, the film that Graham Chapman had spent several years writing and setting up, in collaboration with Bernard McKenna and Peter Cook. A comedy about piracy, it featured Eric Idle, John Cleese and several other comedians including Chapman, Cook and the late Marty Feldman. John Cleese was also closely involved with Michael Blakemore's film of the Royal Shakespeare Company stage hit, *Privates on Parade* by Peter Nichols, and played the role of Major Giles Flack, the blinkered, dim officer in command of a strange entertainment platoon in Malaya in 1948, a bunch of camp variety artistes led by the bizarre, raging homosexual Captain Terry, played by Denis Quilley. Flack is a marvellous Cleese characterisation, a boneheaded, prejudiced, but fundamentally decent English idiot, attempting to establish rapport with his men by speaking to them in outdated slang, and absolutely unaware of the gun-running racket conducted by his sergeant-major under his nose.

Michael Palin is working on the screenplay of another film to be made by Hand-Made, and intends to follow it with one written in collaboration with Terry Jones,

Above, *Graham Chapman shares a trench with Simon, The Holy Man, played by Terry Jones.* Below, *Michael Palin as Pontius Pilate.*

as they continue to explore the film medium. It seems likely that each Python will continue to develop separately, and in view of their individual gifts, will make significant contributions in unexpected areas. Each successive film they have made together has shown a greater assurance of the technique of film-making, and it is their major interest. But the film business is a fickle one, and sustained success remarkably hard to achieve. Even Steven Spielberg, the most successful of all contemporary moviemakers, had a multi-million dollar flop with his *1941*. If and when the Pythons come together in the future for another *Monty Python* movie they will have to choose carefully. But they can, even if they were never to appear together again, regard their massive legacy to modern humour, not merely in Britain, but across the world, and look also to their influence on newer generations of comedians, who have the same respect for them as they once looked to their predecessors such as Spike Milligan. Pythonesque is a word that has found its way into some dictionaries, and the team have occasionally found themselves not only the objects of cult worship, but fodder for certain critics who see in their work correlations between Hegel, Brecht, Rabelais, and the great Geoffrey Chaucer, the fourteenth century's own Monty Python. They are all bright enough to be amused by such intellectual pseudery, and see it as part of the process by which they became a comic institution.

Detractors of Python, and unarguably there are many who have never been able to stomach them, complain that they use humour deliberately to offend, to assault the public with ostentatious displays of bad taste. But what they are really setting out to do, apart from providing a sometimes sublimely crazy level of entertainment, is to open our eyes a little wider, forcing the questioning and close scrutiny of those aspects of life which are generally simply accepted. Through their silliness and absurdity they lead us on to a consideration of ourselves and the state of human existence. It is, perhaps, the most honourable motivation for the clown.

In spite of themselves, the Pythons were awarded the Special Jury Prize for The Meaning of Life *at the 1983 Cannes Film Festival. Elated, they expose themselves in front of the Carlton in the traditional Cannes manner.*

PYTHONOGRAPHY
Compiled by Lucy Douch

TELEVISION

That Was The Week That Was (BBC-1)
1st Series: 24 November 1962 to
 27 April 1963
2nd Series: 28 September 1963 to
 21 December 1963
That Was The Year That Was on
 29 December 1962 and 28 December 1963
Produced and directed by Ned Sherrin.
 Regular cast: David Kernan, Roy Kinnear,
 William Rushton, Kenneth Cope, Lance
 Percival, Millicent Martin, with David
 Frost as linkman. Written contributions
 from **John Cleese.**

Now (TWW)
1966
Teenage pop programme presented by
 Michael Palin.

Frost Report (BBC-1)
1st Series: 10 March 1966 to 28 April 1966
 (1) on Authority (2) on Holidays (3) on Sin
 (4) on Elections (5) on Class (6) on The
 News (7) on Education (8) on Love
2nd Series: 6 April 1967 to 18 May 1967
 (1) on Money (2) on Women (3) on The
 Forces (4) untitled (5) on Parliament (6) on
 The Countryside (7) on Industry
Frost Over Christmas 26 December 1967
Starring David Frost, with Ronnie Barker,
 Ronnie Corbett, **John Cleese,** Sheila
 Steafel, Julie Felix
Written contributions from **John Cleese**
 (material sometimes co-written with
 **Graham Chapman), Michael Palin,
 Terry Jones,** and **Eric Idle.**
Prod James Gilbert.

**Isadora: The Biggest Dancer in the
 World** (BBC-1)
22 September 1966
Starring Vivian Pickles
Produced and directed by Ken Russell
Uncredited appearances by **Michael Palin**
 and **Eric Idle** as members of a jazz band
 playing on the roof of a hearse.

The Late Show (BBC-1)
15 October 1966 to 17 December 1966, and
 5 January 1967 to 1 April 1967
Prod Hugh Burnett (Jack Gold from
 14 January 1967)
Michael Palin and **Terry Jones** wrote
 material and appeared.

The Frost Programme (Rediffusion
 Network)
19 October 1966 to 4 January 1967
Presented by David Frost
Prog Eds **John Cleese,** Tim Brooke-Taylor,
 Bryan Fitzjones, Michael Gowers, Peter
 Baker *Dir* Ian Fordyce *Prod* Geoffrey
 Hughes.

Alice in Wonderland (BBC-1)
28 December 1966
Directed and produced by Jonathan Miller
With Alan Bennett, John Bird, Wilfrid
 Brambell, Peter Cook, Sir John Gielgud,
 Malcolm Muggeridge, Sir Michael
 Redgrave, Peter Sellers and brief,
 uncredited appearance by **Eric Idle.**

At Last the 1948 Show (Rediffusion)
1st Series: 15 February 1967 to
 22 March 1967
2nd Series: 26 September 1967 to
 7 November 1967
Written and performed by Tim Brooke-
 Taylor, **John Cleese, Graham
 Chapman,** Marty Feldman, with Aimi
 Macdonald
Exec Prod David Frost *Dir* Ian Fordyce *Prod
 Eds* **John Cleese** and Tim Brooke-Taylor.

Frost Over England (BBC-1)
26 March 1967
Compilation of Frost Reports for BBC's
 entry for the Montreux Festival 1967,
 including sketches with **John Cleese.**
Additional material by **John Cleese** and
 Graham Chapman.

A Series of Bird's (BBC-1)
3 October 1967 to 21 November 1967
Written by John Bird and John Fortune
Prod Dennis Main Wilson
Additional material by **Michael Palin** and
 Terry Jones.

Twice a Fortnight (BBC-1)
21 October 1967 to 23 December 1967
With Bill Oddie, Jonathan Lynn, Graeme
 Garden and Dilys Watling, plus **Michael
 Palin** and **Terry Jones**
Introduced by Ronald Fletcher. Produced
 and directed by Tony Palmer.

No, That's Me Over Here (Rediffusion
 Network)
14 November 1967 to 19 December 1967
Starring Ronnie Corbett
Written by Barry Cryer, **Graham
 Chapman** and **Eric Idle**
Exec Prod David Frost *Prod* Bill Hitchcock
 and Marty Feldman.

Do Not Adjust Your Set
1st Series: (Rediffusion Network) 4 January
1968 to 28 March 1968
2nd Series: (Thames Television) 19 February
1969 to 14 May 1969
Starring Denise Coffey, **Eric Idle,** David
Jason, **Terry Jones, Michael Palin**
Written by **Eric Idle, Terry Jones** and
Michael Palin with animations by **Terry
Gilliam**
Prod Humphrey Barclay (1st series) Ian
Davidson (2nd series)
Dir Daphne Shadwell (1st series) Adrian
Cooper (2nd series)
Do Not Adjust Your Stocking 26
December 1968.

Marty (BBC-2)
1st Series: 29 April 1968 to 3 June 1968
2nd Series: 9 December 1968 to 13 January
1969
Starring Marty Feldman
Additional material by **John Cleese,
Graham Chapman, Terry Jones** and
Michael Palin (1st series)
Written by **John Cleese** and **Graham
Chapman, Terry Jones** and **Michael
Palin** (2nd series)
Prod Dennis Main Wilson *Dir* Roger Race.

We Have Ways of Making You Laugh
(London Weekend Television)
23 August 1968 to 18 October 1968
Presented by Frank Muir *Prod* Humphrey
Barclay *Dir* Bill Turner
Terry Gilliam resident cartoonist. Written
material and appearances by **Eric Idle.**

Broaden Your Mind (BBC-2)
28 October 1968 to 2 December 1968
Starring Tim Brooke-Taylor and Graeme
Garden
Additional material from **John Cleese,
Graham Chapman, Eric Idle, Terry
Jones** and **Michael Palin**
Guest appearances by **Terry Jones, Michael
Palin** and **Graham Chapman.**

**The Complete and Utter History of
Britain** (London Weekend Television)
12 January 1969 to 16 February 1969
1. From the Dawn of History to the Normal
Conquest
2. Richard the Lionheart to Robin the Hood
3. Edward the First to Richard the Last
4. Perkin Warbeck to Bloody Mary
5. The Great and Glorious Age of Elizabeth
6. James the McFirst to Oliver Cromwell
Starring **Michael Palin** and **Terry Jones**
plus Wallace Eaton, Colin Gordon, Roddy
Maude-Roxby, Melinda Maye and Diana
Quick

Dir Maurice Murphy *Prod* Humphrey
Barclay. Written by **Michael Palin** and
Terry Jones.

Doctor in the House (London Weekend
Television)
12 July 1969
"Why do you want to be a Doctor?" by **John
Cleese** and **Graham Chapman**
Based on the "Doctor" books by Richard
Gordon
Starring Barry Evans *Dir* David Askey *Prod*
Humphrey Barclay.

Monty Python's Flying Circus (BBC-1)
1st Series: 5 October 1969 to 26 October
1969, and 23 November 1969 to 11 January
1970
2nd Series: 15 September 1970 to 29
September 1970, and 20 October 1970 to
22 December 1970
3rd Series: 19 October 1972 to 21 December
1972, and 4 January 1973 to 18 January
1973
Conceived and written by **Graham
Chapman, John Cleese, Eric Idle,
Terry Jones, Michael Palin** and **Terry
Gilliam** *Dir* Ian McNaughton *Prod* John
Howard Davies
Animations by **Terry Gilliam**
4th Series: **Monty Python** (BBC-2) 31
October 1974 to 5 December 1974
Conceived and written by **Graham
Chapman, Terry Gilliam, Eric Idle,
Terry Jones** and **Michael Palin** *Dir* Ian
McNaughton *Prod* John Howard Davies.

Late Night Line Up (BBC-2)
12 January 1970
Presented by Joan Bakewell, Michael Dean,
Tony Bilbow and Sheridan Morley
Ed Rowan Ayers *Prod* Mike Fentiman
Guests: **John Cleese, Graham Chapman,
Terry Gilliam, Eric Idle** and Carol
Cleveland.

The Marty Feldman Comedy Machine
(ATV)
8 October 1971 to 14 January 1972
Dir John Robins *Prod* Larry Gilbert *Exec
Prod* Colin Clews
Animations by **Terry Gilliam.**

Comedy Playhouse (BBC-1)
14 January 1972
"Idle at Work" by **Graham Chapman** and
Bernard McKenna
Starring Ronnie Barker
Prod James Gilbert *Dir* Harold Snoad.

Elementary, My Dear Watson (BBC-1)
Comedy Playhouse 18 January 1973
Written by N.F. Simpson
Starring **John Cleese** as Sherlock Holmes
and William Rushton as Dr Watson
Prod Barry Took *Dir* Harold Snoad.

Doctor at Large/In Charge (London
  Weekend Television)
Various episodes throughout 1972 and 1973
  written by **John Cleese** and co-written
  (with Bernard McKenna/David Sherlock)
  by **Graham Chapman**
Of special interest: "No Ill Feelings" by
  John Cleese, 3 February 1973, featuring
  Timothy Bateson as Basil Fawlty prototype
Dir Alan Wallis *Exec Prod* Humphrey
  Barclay.

Secrets (BBC-2)
Black and Blue drama series, 14 August 1973
Written by **Michael Palin** and **Terry Jones**
Starring Warren Mitchell
Dir James Cellan Jones *Prod* Mark Shivas.

Monty Pythons fliegende Zirkus (BBC-2)
6 October 1973
Special German edition "Schnapps with
  Everything"
Prod Thomas Woitkewitsch of Bavarian
  Atelier GmbH Munich for WDR.

Laughter – Why we Laugh (BBC-1)
14 October 1973
Written and presented by Barry Took, with
  John Cleese, Les Dawson and Peter Black
Prod Vernon Lawrence.

**The Do-It-Yourself Film Animation
  Show** (BBC-1)
5 May 1974
Programme 3: "Table top and cut-out
  animation"
Guest **Terry Gilliam**
Presented by Bob Godfrey *Dir* Anna Jackson
  Prod David Hargreaves.

In Vision (BBC-2)
6 December 1974
William Hardcastle meets Monty Python: a
  look back over five years of Monty
  Python's Flying Circus with some extracts
  from some of the best and worst moments
With **Graham Chapman, Terry Gilliam,
  Terry Jones** and **Michael Palin**
Prod Peter Foges *Ed* Will Wyatt.

Rutland Weekend Television (BBC-2)
1st Series: 12 May 1975 to 16 June 1975
"Christmas with Rutland Weekend
  Television" 26 December 1975
2nd Series: 12 November 1976 to 24
  December 1976
Written by **Eric Idle** *Dir* Andrew Gosling
  Prod Ian Keill
Featuring **Eric Idle,** Neil Innes.

Fawlty Towers (BBC-2)
1st Series: 19 September 1975 to 24 October
  1975
2nd Series: 19 February 1979 to 18 March
  1979, and 25 October 1979
Written by **John Cleese** and Connie Booth
Starring **John Cleese,** Prunella Scales,
  Andrew Sachs and Connie Booth
Prod John Howard Davies (1st series),
  Douglas Argent (2nd series).

The Selling Line (BBC-2) Video Arts Ltd
6 October 1975 to 24 November 1975
Series written by **John Cleese** and Tony Jay
Featuring **John Cleese**
1. Who Sold You This, Then?
2. It's Alright, It's Only a Customer
3. The Competitive Spirit
4. In Two Minds
5. Awkward Customers
6. More Awkward Customers
7. I'll Think About It
8. How Not To Exhibit Yourself.

Three Men in a Boat (BBC-2)
31 December 1975
Screenplay by Tom Stoppard
Starring **Michael Palin,** Tim Curry and
  Stephen Moore
Prod Rosemary Hill *Dir* Stephen Frears.

Tomkinson's Schooldays (BBC-2)
7 January 1976
Written by **Michael Palin** and **Terry Jones**
Produced and directed by Terry Hughes
Starring **Michael Palin,** with **Terry Jones.**

Out of the Trees (BBC-2)
10 January 1976
Featuring **Graham Chapman**
Written by **Graham Chapman,** Bernard
  McKenna, Douglas Adams
Prod Bernard Thompson.

Festival 40 (BBC-1)
16 August 1976
Monty Python's Flying Circus – special
  edition conceived, written and performed
  by **Graham Chapman, John Cleese,
  Terry Gilliam, Eric Idle, Terry Jones**
  and **Michael Palin**

Prod Ian McNaughton
Graham Chapman remembers Monty
Python, interviewed by David Gillard.

Punch Review (BBC-2)
4 January to 15 February 1977
Starring Robin Bailey, Julian Holloway
Including material by **Michael Palin** and
Terry Jones
Prod Roger Race.

Three Piece Suite (BBC-2)
12 April 1977
"Every Day in Every Way" by Alan Coren
with Diana Rigg, **John Cleese**
Prod Michael Mills.

**The Strange Case of the End of
Civilization As We Know It** (London
Weekend Television)
18 September 1977
Written by Jack Hobbs, Joseph McGrath and
John Cleese
Starring **John Cleese** as A. Sherlock-
Holmes, Arthur Lowe and Connie Booth
Dir Joseph McGrath *Prod* Humphrey
Barclay.

Ripping Yarns (BBC-2)
1st Series: 20 September 1977 to 25 October
1977
1. Tomkinson's Schooldays (dir Terry
Hughes)
2. The Testing of Eric Olthwaite (dir Jim
Franklin)
3. Escape from Stalag Luft 112B (dir Terry
Hughes)
4. Murder at Moorstones Manor (dir Terry
Hughes)
5. Across the Andes by Frog (dir Terry
Hughes)
6. The Curse of the Claw (dir Jim Franklin)
2nd Series: 10 October 1979 to 24 October
1979
1. Whinfrey's Last Stand (dir Alan J. W.
Bell)
2. Golden Gordon (dir Alan J. W. Bell)
3. Roger of the Raj (dir Alan J. W. Bell)
Written by **Michael Palin** and **Terry
Jones.**

The Muppet Show (ATV)
21 October 1977
Guest **John Cleese**
Dir Philip Casson *Prod* Jim Henson.

The Rutles (BBC-2)
27 March 1978
Conceived and written by **Eric Idle**
Music and lyrics by Neil Innes. *Dir* Gary
Weis and **Eric Idle**
Featuring **Eric Idle, Michael Palin,** Neil
Innes, Mick Jagger, Ron Wood.

The Pythons (BBC-1)
20 June 1979
Documentary to commemorate the 10th
anniversary of the "best known British
comedy group in the world"
Produced and narrated by Iain Johnstone.

Friday Night, Saturday Morning
(BBC-2)
9 November 1979
Presented by Tim Rice
Discussion between **John Cleese, Michael
Palin,** Malcolm Muggeridge and Dr
Mervyn Stockwood about *Monty Python's
Life of Brian*
Dir John Burrowes *Prod* Iain Johnstone.

The Taming of the Shrew (BBC-2)
23 October 1980
"BBC Television Shakespeare" series
Produced and directed by Jonathan Miller
Starring **John Cleese** and Sarah Badel.

Confessions of a Train-Spotter (BBC-2)
27 November 1980
4th in a series of seven "Great Railway
Journeys of the World"
Featuring **Michael Palin**
Prod Ken Stephinson *Series Prod* Roger
Laughton.

Paperbacks (BBC-1)
3 June 1981 to 15 July 1981
Introduced by **Terry Jones**
Dir Nick Brenton *Prod* Rosemary Bowen-
Jones, Julian Jebb.

The Innes Book of Records (BBC-2)
28 September 1981
Starring Neil Innes
Special guest **Michael Palin**
Prod Ian Keill.

Friday Night ... Saturday Morning
(BBC-2)
6 November 1981
Hosted by **Terry Jones**
Prod Frances Whitaker.

The Rupert Bear Story (Channel Four)
A Tribute to Alfred Bestall
9 December 1982
Dir **Terry Jones** *Prod* Elizabeth Taylor-Mead.

Wogan (BBC-1)
29 January 1983
Hosted by Terry Wogan with **John Cleese**
Prod Marcus Plantin.

Good Morning, Britain (TV-am)
1 February 1983
With **John Cleese** in his pyjamas.

Tim Rice (BBC-1)
16 February 1983
With **Michael Palin**
Prod David F. Turnbull.

Film 83 (BBC-1)
28 February 1983
Barry Norman with **Michael Palin** talking about *The Missionary*
Prod Jane Lush.

Strictly Private (ITV)
3 March 1983
Programme about the making of *Privates on Parade* with **John Cleese**, Denis Quilley, Iain Johnstone.

FILMS

Interlude (1967) *Dir* Kevin Billington
Starring Oscar Werner, Barbara Ferris and Virginia Maskell, with **John Cleese** as a television PR man.

Albert Carter Q.O.S.O. (1968) Dormer Productions
Short film starring Roy Kinnear with **Eric Idle.**

The Magic Christian (1969) *Dir* Joseph McGrath
Starring Peter Sellers and Ringo Starr, with **John Cleese** as a director of Sotheby's and **Graham Chapman** as an Oxford stroke
Screenplay by **Graham Chapman, John Cleese,** Peter Sellers, Terry Southern and Joseph McGrath.

The Rise and Rise of Michael Rimmer (1969) *Dir* Kevin Billington
Starring Vanessa Redgrave, Peter Cook, Denholm Elliott, Ronald Fraser, Arthur Lowe and **John Cleese**
Screenplay by **Graham Chapman, John Cleese,** Peter Cook and Kevin Billington.

The Cry of the Banshee (1970) *Dir* Gordon Hessler
Starring Vincent Price and Elisabeth Bergner, with an uncredited appearance by **Terry Gilliam.**

Doctor in Trouble (1970) *Dir* Ralph Thomas
Starring Leslie Phillips, Harry Secombe and James Robertson Justice, with **Graham Chapman** as Roddy.

The Statue (1970) *Dir* Rod Amateau
Starring David Niven, Virna Lisi, Robert Vaughn and Ann Bell, with **John Cleese** as Harry, a renegade psychiatrist.

And Now For Something Completely Different (1971) *Dir* Ian McNaughton
Written by and featuring **John Cleese, Graham Chapman, Eric Idle, Terry Jones** and **Michael Palin**
Animations by **Terry Gilliam.**

Who's There? (1971) *Dir* Mike Wooler
Instructional film about canvassing produced by the Labour Party
Starring **John Cleese, Graham Chapman, Terry Jones, Michael Palin** and Carol Cleveland.

The Love Ban/It's a 2′ 6″ Above the Ground World (1972) *Dir* Ralph Thomas
Starring Hwyel Bennett, Nanette Newman, Milo O'Shea and **John Cleese.**

Monty Python and the Holy Grail (1974) *Dir* **Terry Jones** and **Terry Gilliam**
Written by and featuring **John Cleese, Graham Chapman, Eric Idle, Terry Jones** and **Michael Palin**
Animations by **Terry Gilliam.**

Romance with a Double Bass (1974) *Dir* Robert Young
Starring **John Cleese** and Connie Booth
Screen adaptation from Chekhov by **John Cleese** with Connie Booth and Robert Young.

The Miracle of Flight (1974) *Dir* **Terry Gilliam**
Short animation.

Pleasure at Her Majesty's (1976) *Dir* Roger Graef
With Alan Bennett, John Bird, Eleanor Bron, Tim Brooke-Taylor, **John Cleese,** Peter Cook, Bill Oddie, John Fortune, **Michael Palin** and **Terry Jones.**

Jabberwocky (1977) *Dir* **Terry Gilliam**
Starring **Michael Palin** as Dennis Cooper,
Max Wall, John le Mesurier, Warren
Mitchell and Harry H. Corbett, with
Terry Jones as a poacher.

The Odd Job (1978) *Dir* Peter Medak
Starring **Graham Chapman** as Arthur
Harris, and David Jason
Written and co-produced by **Graham
Chapman.**

Monty Python's Life of Brian (1979) *Dir*
Terry Jones
Written by and featuring **John Cleese,
Graham Chapman, Eric Idle, Terry
Jones** and **Michael Palin** with **Terry
Gilliam.**

The Secret Policeman's Ball (1979) *Dir*
Roger Graef
With Rowan Atkinson, Ken Campbell, **John
Cleese,** Peter Cook, **Michael Palin,** Pete
Townshend, John Williams, **Terry Jones**
Stage direction by **John Cleese.**

Away From It All (1979) *Dir* Clare Taylor,
John Cleese
Narrated by Nigel Farquar-Bennet **(John
Cleese)**

The Great Muppet Caper (1981) *Dir* Jim
Henson
Starring Charles Grodin, Diana Rigg with
John Cleese.

Time Bandits (1981) *Dir* **Terry Gilliam**
Starring Sean Connery, Shelley Duvall, Ian
Holm, **John Cleese,** David Warner and
Craig Warnock
Screenplay by **Terry Gilliam** and **Michael
Palin.**

The Secret Policeman's Other Ball
(1982) *Dir* Julien Temple
With Rowan Atkinson, Alan Bennett,
Graham Chapman, John Cleese, Billy
Connolly, John Fortune, Alexei Sayle,
Pamela Stephenson, John Wells
Guest appearance by **Michael Palin.**

The Missionary (1982) *Dir* Richard
Loncraine
Exec prods George Harrison, Denis O'Brien
Co-prods **Michael Palin,** Neville C.
Thompson
Starring **Michael Palin,** Maggie Smith,
Trevor Howard, Michael Hordern.

**Monty Python Live At The Hollywood
Bowl** (1982) *Dir* Terry Hughes
Written and performed by **Graham
Chapman, John Cleese, Terry Gilliam,
Eric Idle, Terry Jones** and **Michael
Palin**
With Carol Cleveland, Neil Innes, Pamela
Stephenson.

Monty Python's Meaning of Life (1983)
Dir **Terry Jones**
Director of animation and special sequences:
Terry Gilliam
Written and performed by **Graham
Chapman, John Cleese, Terry Gilliam,
Eric Idle, Terry Jones** and **Michael
Palin.**

Privates On Parade (1983) *Dir* Michael
Blakemore
Starring **John Cleese,** Denis Quilley,
Michael Elphick.

Yellowbeard (1983) *Dir* Mel Damski
Screenplay by **Graham Chapman,** Bernard
McKenna, Peter Cook
Starring **Graham Chapman, John Cleese,
Eric Idle,** Cheech and Chong, Madeline
Kahn, Peter Cook, Marty Feldman.

BOOKS

Monty Python's Big Red Book Methuen 1971

The Brand New Monty Python Bok Methuen
1973 (issued in paperback as *The Brand
New Monty Python Papperbok*/Methuen
1974).

Monty Python and the Holy Grail (*Book*)
Edited by **Terry Jones**/Designed by Derek
Birdsall/Methuen 1977

Monty Python's Life of Brian Edited by **Eric
Idle**/Designed by Basil Pao/Methuen 1979

*The Complete Works of Shakespeare and
Monty Python: Volume One – Monty
Python* Methuen 1981 (combined reissue of
Monty Python's Big Red Book and *The
Brand New Monty Python Bok*)

Bert Fegg's Nasty Book for Boys and Girls
Terry Jones and **Michael Palin**/
Methuen 1974

Rutland Dirty Weekend Book **Eric Idle**/
Methuen 1976

Hello Sailor **Eric Idle**/Futura 1976

The Strange Case of the End of Civilization as We Know It **John Cleese** and Jack Hobbs/ Star Books 1977

Fawlty Towers **John Cleese** and Connie Booth/Contact Publications 1977

Animations of Mortality **Terry Gilliam**/ Methuen 1978

Ripping Yarns **Terry Jones** and **Michael Palin**/Methuen 1978

Fawlty Towers Book 2 **John Cleese** and Connie Booth/Weidenfeld and Nicolson 1979

More Ripping Yarns **Terry Jones** and **Michael Palin**/Methuen 1980

A Liar's Autobiography **Graham Chapman**/Methuen 1980

Chaucer's Knight – the Portrait of a Medieval Mercenary **Terry Jones**/Weidenfeld and Nicolson 1980

Fairy Tales **Terry Jones**/Illustrated by Michael Foreman/Pavilion Books 1981

Time Bandits: A Screenplay **Michael Palin** and **Terry Gilliam**/Hutchinson 1981

The Missionary **Michael Palin**/Methuen 1982

Pass the Butler **Eric Idle**/Methuen 1982

Small Harry and the Toothache Pills **Michael Palin**/Methuen 1982

Monty Python's The Meaning of Life Methuen 1983

Families and How to Survive them **John Cleese** and Robin Skynner/Methuen 1983

The Saga of Erik the Viking **Terry Jones**/ Illustrated by Michael Foreman/Pavilion Books 1983

RECORDS

Monty Python's Flying Circus
1970/BBC Records/REB 73M

Another Monty Python Record
1971/Charisma/CAS 1049

Monty Python's Previous Record
1972/Charisma/CAS 1063

The Monty Python Matching Tie And Handkerchief
1973/Charisma/CAS 1080

Monty Python Live At Drury Lane
1974/Charisma/Class 4

The Album Of The Soundtrack Of The Trailer Of The Film Of Monty Python And The Holy Grail
1975/Charisma/CAS 1103

The Rutland Weekend Songbook
1975/BBC Records/REB 233

A Poke In The Eye With A Sharp Stick
1976/Transatlantic/TRA 331
Recording of the 1976 Amnesty Show with **Graham Chapman, John Cleese, Terry Gilliam, Terry Jones, Michael Palin,** Carol Cleveland, Neil Innes, Alan Bennett, John Bird, Eleanor Bron, Tim Brooke-Taylor, Peter Cook

Monty Python Live At City Center
1976/Kay Gee Bee Songs Inc/AB 4073
Recording of stage show at City Center, New York

Mermaid Frolics
1977/Polydor/2384101
Recording of the 1977 Amnesty Show with **John Cleese, Terry Jones,** Connie Booth, Julie Covington, Jonathan Miller, Peter Ustinov, The Bowles Brothers

The Monty Python Instant Record Collection
1977/Charisma/CAS 1134

The Rutles: All You Need Is Cash
1978/Warner Bros/K 56459

Fawlty Towers
1979/BBC Records/REB 377

The Secret Policeman's Ball
1979/Island/ILPS 9601

Monty Python's Life Of Brian
1979/Warner Bros/K 56751

Monty Python's Contractual Obligation Album
1980/Charisma/CAS 1152

Fawlty Towers: Second Sitting
1981/BBC Records/REB 405

The Secret Policeman's Other Ball
1981/Island/HAHA 6003

Fawlty Towers At Your Service
1982/BBC Records/REB 449

VIDEO CASSETTES

The Magic Christian/Video Forum

Monty Python And The Holy Grail/Brent
Walker Video

Monty Python's Life Of Brian/Thorn
EMI Video

The Secret Policeman's Ball/Hokushin

The Great Muppet Caper/Precision Video

Time Bandits/Thorn EMI Video

The Secret Policeman's Other Ball/
Videospace Ltd

**Monty Python Live At The Hollywood
Bowl**/Thorn EMI Video

Plus training films featuring **John Cleese**
from Video Arts

PICTURE CREDITS

Amnesty International: p. 169; BBC Picture Publicity: 11, 12, 13, 14, 23, 36, 44 (bottom R.), 45 (centre), 59 (top), 73 (centre), 79 (top L., centre and bottom), 86 (right), 87 (top L. and R.), 96, 97, 100 (top R. and bottom L.), 101 (bottom), 112 (top), 120 (centre), 121, 125 (bottom), 127, 130/131, 142 (bottom), 149 (bottom R.); Humphrey Barclay Collection: 18, 28, 29, 31 (bottom L. and cartoon), 38 (bottom), 39 (bottom), 42 (top), 44 (top L. and bottom centre), 50, 51, 58 (top R.), 91, 92, 93, 109 (L.), 113 (top R.), 116, 118; Columbia: 81 (bottom), 129 (bottom R.), 160 (bottom), 176 (bottom), 177, 178, 184; Zoë Dominic: 20 (inset); HandMade Films: 55 (bottom), 82, 85, 86 (L.), 124 (centre), 164, 165 (top), 174; Robert Hewison: 33, 34, 35, 64, 65; Neil Innes: 120 (top), Keystone: 15 (top); LWT: 41, 42 (bottom), 43, 58 (bottom), 72 (bottom), 80; Mander & Mitchenson: 16 (top), 22; Lewis Morley: 24 (top); National Film Archive: 15 (bottom), 37, 55 (top), 73 (top L.), 100 (bottom R.), 101 (top L.), 124 (top), 128, 159, 160 (top), 161, 173, 176 (top); National Gallery: 79 (top R.); Newark Advertiser: 117; Orion Pictures: 101 (top R.); Pavilion Books: 68; Popperfoto: 16 (bottom); Python Productions: 2, 5; Radio Times (Don Smith) 122, 133, 134, 135, 136, 137, 138, 139, 140, 141, 142 (top and centre), 143, 144, 145, 146, 147, 148, 149 (bottom L.), 152, 153, 154, 155; Rex Features: 53, 99; Thames Television: 39 (top), 113 (bottom R.); Time Out: 44 (top R.); Universal City Studios Inc: 8, 44 (bottom L.), 45 (top L.), 59 (bottom L.), 73 (top R.), 100 (top L.), 112 (bottom), 113 (top L.), 124 (bottom), 125 (top), 180; Video Arts: 87 (centre).